Gardens OF Illusion

Gardens
of Illusion

PLACES OF WIT AND ENCHANTMENT

Sara Maitland and Peter Matthews

CASSELL&CO

For Kate Smith and for Catherine Hull

First published in the United Kingdom in 2000 by Cassell & Co
Text copyright © Sara Maitland and Peter Matthews, 2000
Design and layout copyright © Cassell & Co, 2000

Distributed in the United States of America by
Sterling Publishing Co., Inc.
387 Park Avenue South
New York
NY 10016 - 8810

A CIP catalogue record for this book is available from the British Library

ISBN 0304 35434 1
Art Director David Rowley
Editorial Director Catherine Bradley
Designed by Nigel Soper
Edited by Slaney Begley
Picture research by Helen Fickling and Marissa Keating
Index by Drusilla Calvert

Typeset in Bembo
Printed and Bound in Spain

Cassell & Co
Wellington House
125 Strand
London WC2R 0BB

Contents

Introduction

GARDENS OF ILLUSION is a book about gardens we like. It is not a book about garden design, nor horticultural know-how; it describes the way we think about gardens. We have come to believe that, what with concerns about 'good taste' (which mainly means fashion), our obsession with blooms, with coloured flowers, and the four-century-long debate about the 'natural' versus the 'formal', we have stopped thinking very creatively about gardens – what they are for, what we want them to do for us, and how we use them.

In case this sounds terribly earnest and high minded, we hasten to assure you that we have come to the conclusion that what gardens are *for* is having fun. Of course what is fun for one person is a nightmare for another – for everyone who thinks that the practical joke is the most hilarious social event imaginable, there is another who feels nauseous at the very idea and whose idea of fun is listening to Bach sonatas. In a sense that is the point – our 'philosophy' is based on the idea that people's gardens should be more different from each other than they are, because people have such different interests and emotional responses. However, there are very few people whose idea of fun is admiring someone else's perfect begonias – this is worth bearing in mind.

We have known each other for a quarter of a century (which actually means that we have known each other since Peter was one year old); for the last eight years we have spent a lot of time together looking at, talking about and thinking on gardens. This is where our book began.

Increasingly, we found we were bored by a great many gardens. The so-called 'natural' gardens seemed bogus. The 'cottage garden' look had run its course. Elsewhere the choices seemed to fall between ill-considered plantings in garish hues (worst of all in show gardens that seemed to specialize in highly forced arrangements that no gardener at home could possibly replicate) and a kind of modernist sterility that would prove equally impractical, either due to expense and planning regulations or because it would be impossible to live with. There are, of course, a great many exceptions to this sweeping condemnation, many of which will be mentioned in this book.

When we asked ourselves why this was the case – given that more varieties of plants, more equipment and more materials are available now than ever before – we came to the conclusion that gardens were no longer required to express the wider personality of the gardener. Instead, they were expected to conform to a fashion for lots and lots of flowers and a concept of 'good taste' that suppressed individuality, risk and above all wit – both humour and the demonstration of a quirky high-spirited and individual intelligence. Somehow, over the last century or so, wit has been banished from the garden. It has been

Above

Many artworks have been incorporated seamlessly into the layout of the Gibberd Garden in Essex. Here, Coiled Pot *by Monica Young nestles under the twisted branches of an old quince tree, creating a composition that is perfectly at one with the garden.*

replaced by some rather odd ideas about what it is to be natural. But as we argue, the one thing that a garden cannot be is 'natural'.

The word 'wit' is double-edged. It means humour and it means 'quick witted', intelligent (as in 'having all you wits about you') in a particularly sociable and allusive way. The sorts of gardens that came to interest us most were the ones that showed both these meanings of wit. A mixture of light-hearted, almost childlike, delight and a creative, informed, open-minded thoughtfulness.

We began to talk about this sort of garden – places that were fun, surprising, witty and, because of the very nature of wit, highly individual. And as soon as we started thinking, we started seeing too. There were lots of people doing extraordinary things in their gardens, often very individual and private, although sometimes supported by wonderful witty designers. The scale could vary from the 12 hectares (30 acres) of Charles Jencks' Garden of Cosmic Speculation, which involves earthworks on the Silbury Hill and Stonehenge level, through to very small gardens such as Judy Wiseman's with its 'birds' nest' and 'planted' resin noses and fingers. Size, budget, climate and situation seem to be irrelevant. There are witty, magical gardens all over the place though they are largely unsung and little known.

Above

Often, the unexpected can be just as effective in provoking a response as the contrived. This old tree stump has been given a new lease of life and provides a startling focal point to a long vista.

What makes a witty garden? *Nerve.* The courage to break away from expectation and follow a personal vision – backed up by a willingness to think, to establish a point of reference, and to learn the specific skills that the vision requires. All the courage in the world will not be enough, however, unless it is accompanied by a lack of earnestness. We should not take ourselves or our gardens too seriously. They are just gardens after all. We have fallen into a rather precious habit of solemnity. A garden is not a church (though it would be nice if more churches were like gardens): the only purpose of a garden is delight; a witty garden is one where horticultural skill, imagination, creativity and intelligence have been directed towards pleasure. It cannot be pompous, self-important or trying to impress.

Why don't more people have witty gardens? The answer to this question turned out to be complex – and looking for answers we turned to the history of gardening. We discovered that when, with the European Renaissance, garden design really commenced, gardens were expected to be both surprising and thought-provoking; they were witty, tricky, allusive and reflected the ideas and interests of their owners. This somehow got lost in the following four centuries while the argument between the 'formal' and the 'natural' raged on, and the development of a wider range of flowers occupied the minds of many of the best horticulturists. We have begun our book with a historical chapter about these early understandings of gardens because we think that what we are looking for is both highly novel and very traditional.

One of the things we learned was how much our gardening ancestors were interested in the relationship between civilization and nature, and how gardens were expected to reflect that relationship. Today, our gardens are still, consciously or unconsciously, one of the main places where we work out that relationship, and this has made us think about location and views and privacy and ownership – all those things that explain what we mean by, and like about, landscape.

However, in essence what we did was to look at gardens that pleased us, and talk to the gardeners who made them. Some of them are professional garden designers, but more are people working on their own gardens for their private, very personal, pleasure.

On the whole we noticed that there are two sorts of witty garden: the ones that make you laugh and the ones that enchant you. It is a fairly arbitrary division because lots of gardens do both – and both always have an element of surprise – but for our, and we hope your, convenience we needed to break them up further into various types of witty garden.

We have started with the theme of laughter – with garden jokes, with wit in its most basic sense. We have already pointed out that what one person finds funny another will find silly or tasteless, so this is a highly personal chapter. You may learn more about us than about gardens from it!

Wit also carries with it an element of trickery, of illusion or even magic. The oldest garden illusion is the way a pool of still water reflects and pretends to be a whole new world. So in the next chapter we explore ideas of reflection, in the physical sense, in water, mirrors and other surfaces. This leads us on to the ancient idea that gardens were meant to support mental reflection; that they were places to meditate, think and bounce ideas about; places to use all one's wits.

Then we have tackled ideas about enchantment – about magic. Some readers may feel that the magic of gardens is a magic of nature and can have nothing to do with artifice, trickery and illusion, but we disagree profoundly and hope that the next chapter will explain why. Although it is easier to create a sense

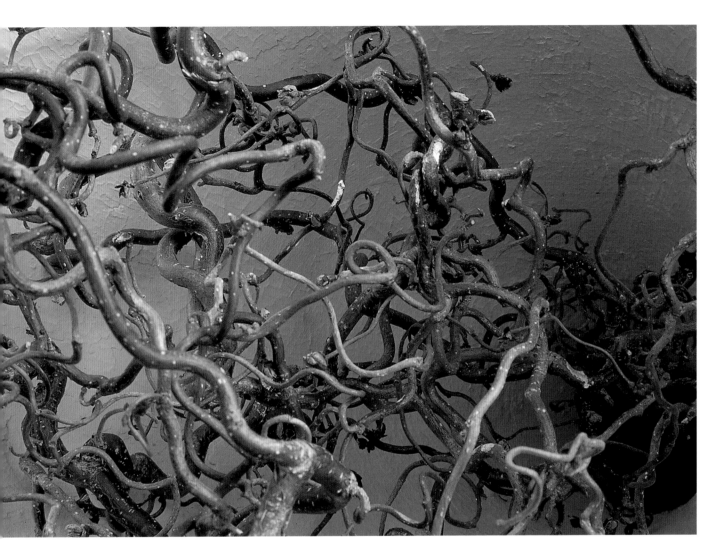

of enchantment in a large, country retreat, we also hope to show how some gardeners have brought magic into even the smallest and most restricted town garden.

And finally we consider wit in the sense of a flexible intelligence and look at people who have used their gardens to express ideas, passions and hobbies that have nothing to do with gardening. In this chapter we discovered that the people who do this best often have learned about horticulture at an expert level in order to use plants or trees to express their ideas, just as a great artist in any medium must understand how his or her materials work and how to use them.

We have also looked at individual garden features and ideas. At the end of the book we have outlined some directions or techniques. There are a number of design and craft activities which may seem dauntingly difficult or expensive, but which in fact are far simpler than they appear. This final section is meant to offer advice and encouragement, not to make experts out of you.

Because of our emphasis we have been accused of being anti-plants. This is unfair. We are pro-gardens and plantless gardens that satisfy their owners are few and far between, though they do exist. But we all know we can grow flowers, we need to ask ourselves what we are going to do with them. In this book we treat flowers as one of the things you can put in a garden, they are garden furniture or garden features

Above

In the Garden in Mind in Sussex, Ivan Hicks has created a garden based on Surrealist thought and Celtic numerology. The garden is dotted with compositions that work as abstracts as well as part of the whole. Here, curved twigs serve to represent 'sound' emanating from an old gramophone horn.

of a special kind. Most people will want to have them in their gardens, and for some people the science of gardening will be what draws them on, will be their wit and magic. But we are all obsessed with flowers, despite the fact that there are lots of other things we might be putting in and doing to our gardens. To be honest, we want plants for their effect, not for their name tag. Very few of our friends are going to be struck with awe because of the subtle difficulty of bringing to flower in alkaline soil a very rare acid-preferring species, or are even going to notice a precious rarity in our borders. A truly blue rose might move some of them, but we doubt that a blue tulip would; it wouldn't move us much, actually, unless we had bred it ourselves – a journey neither of us is planning to set out on. Perhaps, in this place, in this garden, a blue cornflower, anchusa, or delphinium might do just as well. So might a blue-painted stone, come to that. Garden centres, which have done so much to put once rare species and cultivars within the reach of ordinary gardeners, also have a lot to answer for – things in flower sell better, so that is what they offer, celebrate and make popular or fashionable. All gardeners who have ever criticized expensive-trainer-sporting teenagers for being 'fashion victims' should look around the garden and ask whether they have fallen into the same trap.

Doing the research for this book has been enormous fun. One stunningly beautiful June day we were driving through the Lake District, *en route* from one wonderful garden to another. We looked at each other and just laughed, and Peter said: 'And this is work!!' But the main reason it was such a fabulous project was because of the extraordinary generosity, kindness and support of so many gardeners, who gave us their time, access to their gardens, their ideas and their knowledge (and their tea and coffee and more). Good, imaginative, creative gardeners seem to be extraordinarily lovely people. Although there is no moral edification intended in our approach to gardening, it is worth noticing that you may well become more lovable as you become more witty. We have listed those whose gardens are open to the public, but we also want to thank deeply those who do not, for whatever reasons, want to be named.

This is a deeply biased book that makes no claims to being prescriptive or comprehensive. We are not ashamed of this, partly because although we have visited over 100 gardens we are well aware that there are many more that we have not seen (either because we did not have the opportunity or because we did not know they were there) and partly because we believe that gardening 'fashion' has got in the way of gardening 'wit', and the latter *has* to be based strongly on individual tastes and ideas; it cannot be prescribed. All we can do really is to liberate imaginations and encourage boldness. And these qualities will always be a bit risky – walking boldly means walking on the boundaries of what is understood as 'good taste'. Yet in the end this is about having fun. Yes, it is risky. Fashionable decorum is safer, earnest high-mindedness is risk free. What we are suggesting is that first of all it is surprising how often the results are worth the risk. And secondly that it is only a garden – it really does not matter that much. Who needs to be earnest in paradise?

Above
Anne Wareham's garden in Monmouthshire raises many subtle questions. These mosaic fish are not in the pool, but still seem to be swimming. When walking in this garden, one is continually asking, 'What is natural?'

Opposite
The spiral staircase in the Whitehursts' garden is a magical feature that leads to a fairy-tale walk through the tree tops.

The Wit Tradition

*I beautyfied the same with Ornaments of contemplative
Groves and Walks, as well as artificial Thunder and
Lightning, Rain, Hail-showers, Drums beating, Organs
playing, Birds singing, Water murmuring, the Dead arising,
Lights moving, Rainbows reflecting with the beams of the
Sun, and watery showers springing from the same Fountain.*

THOMAS BUSHELL (1594–1674)

BUSHELL is writing almost ecstatically about the 'Delicate Grotto' that he constructed at Enstone, in Oxfordshire, in the 1620s.[1] He had moved to the area near Charlbury in 1620 and had the good luck to find a cave in a hillside, already festooned with stalactites – 'pendants like icecles' as he called them. He quickly developed this with the mechanical devices, statuary and ornamentation he describes here, plus a number of joke fountains that squirted or dribbled on his visitors, apparently to everyone's delight and amusement. Above the grotto he constructed a small house, in which his study was draped in black fabric 'representing a melancholy retyr'd life like a hermit' and in his bedroom the bed floated from the ceiling on cords 'instead of bed postes'. Around his grotto Bushell designed a small garden with yet more walks and 'contemplative groves' where he, accompanied by musicians, could 'walke all night'. It was a place that encouraged contemplation, meditation in solitude or philosophic conversation in social company.

Bushell was no hermit, nor isolated eccentric. The 'Enstone marvels' were much admired in their day and the garden received two royal visits in the 1630s. There are several different descriptions of its delights – but what is interesting both in this quotation, and in almost all the writing about it, is that there is virtually no mention of flowers. Apart from a reasonable assumption that the 'neat walkes' and groves were planted with trees, we are forced to assume that either there were no flowers or that they were entirely incidental to the architectural and mechanical aspects of the plan.

He was not alone in this concept of the garden. All his contemporaries would have agreed that a garden should be as constructed, as 'unnatural', as artistic, as the house itself: more so in many ways, because here the owner could give way to his more extravagant fancies, while the house had to function in a complex social milieu where issues of private and public had yet to be fully worked out. The design constraints of a house were rigorous, whereas at this time a *garden* was well established within the private and personal sphere. Here the owner owed nothing to duty, or public estate, but only to himself, his elevation and self-development. The garden was more like the work of a modern poet than that of a 21st-century horticulturist.

Opposite

*At the Villa Garzoni in
Italy, evidence of a long
tradition of humour, wit
and personal expression in
the garden can be seen in
this canine grotto that
lurks beneath the formal
balustrading.*

Bushell's design was driven by strongly intellectual ideas. His inspiration was drawn from various sources, both scientific and aesthetic – the gardens at the Villa d'Este and Pratolino in Italy, and Salomon de Caus' treatise on hydraulic engineering for example; as well as literary and philosophical works such as English poet Sir Philip Sidney's *Arcadia* and the writings of 1st century AD Greek mathematician Hero of Alexandria. But above all, as Bushell himself acknowledged, his primary point of reference was the gardens and garden writing of Francis Bacon, Viscount St Albans. His grotto was designed 'in imitation of that excellent Lord's sublime fancy'.

Bushell was a favourite secretary to Francis Bacon. When Bacon, as an important political and intellectual figure and senior public servant, had wandered, meditating, through his own newly constructed gardens at Gorhambury in Hertfordshire, Bushell was 'attending him with his pen and ink horn to set down his present notions.' Bacon was a man of immense and wide learning – the three gardens that he designed and built were only a tiny part of his cultural, literary, political, philosophic and professional (legal) life. Born in 1561, the eighth child of a well-connected family that nevertheless could not afford an independence to all the young generation, Francis Bacon had a prolonged struggle to establish himself under Queen Elizabeth, but with the succession of James I he rose rapidly in the Civil Service and in 1618 became Lord Chancellor and was given the peerage of St Albans. In 1621, however, he was found guilty of taking bribes – and his sentence included disqualification from public office. He retired to the country to write philosophy and perform scientific experiments until his death in 1626. Throughout his life he maintained a wide acquaintance and travelled throughout the country – he corresponded on gardening as well as other matters with his relative Robert Cecil. His ideas about garden design and horticultural science, known to us through *Of Gardens* (1625) and sections V and VI of *Sylva sylvarum* (post 1626) were not flamboyant eccentricities, but based on his own lifetime of gardening activities and on the experience and practice of his friends. Although *Of Gardens* is an individual and personal essay on taste and beauty, there is nothing to suggest that its underlying ideas were not those in fashion during the first half of the 17th century.

The garden was not meant to reflect nature. It was meant to reflect social life; it was art, which along with all his contemporaries Bacon would have understood as something more akin to 'artful' than to the free-flowing self-exploration and self-expression which the Romantic movement of the late 18th and early 19th centuries have given it. Consciously and deliberately, gardens were supposed to reflect the victory of civilization over nature: they should represent philosophical and scientific progress, abstract ideas and social intercourse. The designing and making of a garden was first and foremost an intellectual project.

Many of the key points that Bacon made in *Of Gardens* may seem quite strange now. In the first place he clearly saw the garden as part of the house, rather than part of the countryside. For Bacon the social and architectural needs of the garden were paramount. He recommended, for instance, a 'place of shade' in the 'under story [of the house] towards the garden' – functioning, one imagines, like a contemporary

Below

Although their main influences were those of Islam, the makers of the Generalife in Spain shared many of Bacon's design ideals. These included the continuous presence and sound of water, covered walkways and pavilions from which guests could survey the garden.

conservatory, even though we feel more need to capture sunshine than shade. The garden had to contain a number of elements that would aid social life: there must be a raised mound in the centre for a banqueting hall; a profusion of covered walks and alleys; plus pavilions – ideally raised so that guests could survey the garden – mazes, fountains and summerhouses.

He wanted a layout that was formal and geometrical; from the central mound the garden should be symmetrical, designed in interlinked circles and squares. It should be hidden from the outside world by hedges. Some of these, he advised, should be built up into 'green architecture' with wooden-framed pillars and small turrets surmounted by bird cages. He wanted architectural topiary – pyramids and columns – although he was less keen on representational topiary, apparently thinking beasts and such were a little vulgar.

In *Of Gardens* Bacon was adamant about the management of water features.

For fountains, they are a great beauty and refreshment, but pools mar all and make the garden unwholesome and full of flies and frogs. Fountains I intend to be of two natures – the one that sprinkleth or spouteth water; the other a fair receipt [pool] of water some 30 or 40 foot square, but without fish or slime or mud. For the first the ornament of images, gilt or of marble, which are in use, do well, but the main matter is so to convey the water that it never stay either in the bowls or in the cistern, that the water be never, by rest, discoloured green or red or the like, or gather any mossiness or putrefaction. Besides that it is to be cleaned every day by the hand.... The bottom be finely paved and with images; the sides likewise; and withal embellished with coloured glass and such things of lustre.

Although there seems to have been no water at Twickenham, his first garden, Bacon became fascinated by water. When he moved to Gorhambury in 1620 he felt so strongly that he could not develop his garden without water, of which there was a complete absence around the house, that he declared, 'If the water could not be brought to the house we would bring the house to the water.' He moved the gardens, and subsequently built a new home, Verulam House, about 1.6 kilometres (1 mile) from the original one so that he could use some old monastic fishponds for his schemes. He ended up with a 1.6-hectare (4-acre) water garden that included a central island with a 'curious banqueting house of Roman architecture' surrounded by geometrical walks and hedges. He wanted this island to be encircled by several smaller satellite islands each distinctively ornamented with plants or statues. But this was to be no naturalistic lake: he practised as he preached. As we have seen he was opposed to anything associated with murk or stagnation and the bottom of his lake was decorated with painted or gravel set pictures (John Aubrey mentions images of fish) or patterns that would entertain visitors and emphasize the *unnatural* clarity of the water, as well as reflect the classical Roman uses of mosaics. Aubrey commented that he became so keen on these paved ponds that 'if a poor bodie had brought his lordship half a dozen pebbles of a curious colour he would give them a shilling so curious was he in perfecting his fish ponds.'[2]

In short he wanted a garden in which nature was used, contained, and managed. Even his proposed *heath*, or *natural wilderness*, designed as the furthest barrier between the garden and the outside world, was to have carefully pruned shrubs and artificial hillocks and mounds. And he wanted all this not in order to show off his horticultural skills, although these were considerable and creative, but to entertain his guests, aid conversation and extend the space of his home. He praises his own first garden at Twickenham Park, which he leased from 1594 until 1606, by saying that he 'found the situation of that place much convenient for the trial of my philosophical conclusions'. A garden was Art in the sense that pictures hang on walls, rather than in the craft sense of growing a weed-free lawn. A garden for him was another reception room; both art objects – statuary for example – and clever mechanical devices were integral to that vision.

In garden design, as elsewhere, Bacon was no radical, but a pretty sober man and his garden schemes reflect that. Across Europe gardens were being built that incorporated extravagances that he might have faltered before: entire hunts clipped in topiary, fountains that squirted at guests, artificial birds that sang and gurgled, banqueting halls perched on artificial mounds, elaborate visual jokes – mazes, arbours and bowers specifically designed for romantic assignations.

To his contemporaries, there was nothing remarkable about any of Bacon's suggestions in the area of design. (When it came to horticulture he was far bolder, taking a scientific and experimental approach to a number of issues, including germination, fertilizers, the different amounts of shade and water that suited different species, and how to speed up or retard flowering.) His instructions about formality, sociability and, most importantly, how artifice – both witty and intellectual – should dominate nature in the garden merely articulated an understanding of gardening towards which England, like the rest of Europe, had been moving for as long as we have any garden records. This is not surprising: gardening, agriculture itself – now generally held to be the very point of departure for human culture and social development – is necessarily opposed to the natural. Until this century no one would have thought that a garden should represent nature, but precisely the reverse.

As Europe settled down after the upheavals of the Reformation and the tensions around the discovery of the New Worlds (both west and east) the cult of civilized domesticity asserted itself throughout the continent. The making of gardens became a fashionable pursuit, and so did travelling: for the first time there was a wide cross-fertilization between the different traditions within Europe. The gardens that the travellers were seeing in Europe, and that the writers were imagining, tended to be highly structured and highly intellectual; they were meant to reflect classical and contemporary scientific ideas. Sir Philip Sidney (1554–86) travelled to Italy and was enormously influenced by the gardens he saw there. In the early 1580s he wrote the *Arcadia* (published in 1590, but in private circulation before that), a sort of courtly romance or early novel, which became a bestseller. His description of gardens in it influenced real gardens as well as ideas about gardens for his generation. At one point he describes a garden that surrounded a star-shaped lodge and spread out in geometrical array 'not unlike a fair comet'. The ornamentation of the garden consisted partly of hydraulic toys: an artificial rainbow, a table that revolved and mechanical birds that sang. Sidney's sources of inspiration for this fantasy were numerous. The siting of the lodge and garden is drawn almost directly from the Roman writer Pliny's description of the ideal location for a country house. The description of the lodge seems to be modelled on the Palazzo Farnese at Caprarola, and the

Above

Contemporary with the Villa d'Este, the Villa Lante also has an extravagance of water in line with the thinking of the time. The garden is built on a hillside, and cascades are used to enhance its main axes.

PRATOLINO

hydraulic works may well have been influenced by the Villa d'Este at Tivoli, which Sidney never visited but would certainly have heard of, and which themselves were derived from a work by Hero of Alexandria.

These sorts of ideas were being practised in the gardens of the rich. Philip Sidney's sister, Mary, Countess of Pembroke, created a garden based explicitly on ideas about the Garden of Eden – including 'a deal of intricate setting … every way curiously and chargeably conceited … resembling both divine and moral remembrances, as three arbours standing in a triangle … a greater arbour in the midst resembleth three in one and one in three.' Thomas Tresham, locked up in prison for his recusant activities, beguiled his time designing fantasy pavilions and summerhouses that represented his faith: the Triangular Lodge in Rushden (in which the poor rabbit warrener had to live) followed Mary Pembroke in symbolizing the Trinity, and the New Beeld near Oundle – a three-storied pavilion – is not only cruciform but also carved with symbolic motifs of the passion of Christ. The New Beeld overlooked a complex garden, a moated square and with four mounds at its corners, but sadly no details of its actual internal design remain.

Within these highly philosophical gardens there was always room for a more cheerful sort of wit. In the late 16th century Bernardo Buontalenti built a garden for Francesco I de Medici at Pratolino that contained many *meraviglie* (marvels) including mechanical – almost entirely hydraulic – jokes and devices. Francesco was a complex character. Among his abiding interests were science and alchemy, and despite his onerous public duties he had what amounted to an obsession with personal privacy. To meet these various desires, Buontalenti (who interestingly had begun life as a theatrical set designer) built the garden as a series of highly allusive intellectual mini-gardens – a sort of Renaissance version of John Brookes' garden rooms. In one garden, called The Fountain of the Flood (or the Grotto of the Tritons), he produced

Above
Within the highly intellectual gardens of the time, there was always room for a more lighthearted turn of wit. The celebrated garden at Pratolino, near Florence, included many mechanical jokes and devices.

At the Villa Beatrice, in Florence, the humorous perspective is taken a step further with this 'classical' statue framed by the undergrowth.

trick thunder, lightning and rainbows. In another, Pan piped and in response to the music a nymph rose out of a reed bed, while an automated swan dipped its head in and out of the water and Galatea rode by on a shell-shaped barge. Elsewhere, there were working models of a knife sharpener, a blacksmith's forge, an oil press, and a larger than life-sized washer woman wringing out a cloth into a large pool. Francesco's desire for privacy was met, in The Grotto of the Samaritan, by a dining room in which the guests were served by automata – a mechanized stone statue poured water for them to wash; an elaborate system of wheels brought food from the kitchen; and within the jasper table surface were lids, under each of which a fountain delivered fresh water to each of the guests. Every now and then, heralded by artificial bird song and bagpipe music, an automaton of a woman would enter, draw water from a well and depart, while above her a mechanical hunt pursued its course. There was also a grotto of love, where cupid swung round to face visitors and shot a jet of water instead of an arrow at them, and what would now be called a tree-house, with a spiral staircase leading up a live oak tree to a platform that overlooked a constructed Mount of Parnassus containing a hydraulic organ. And this, unbelievably, is a pruned and truncated selection of just a few of the features.

Tastes change inevitably, but this idea of the garden broadly continued even when the way it was expressed altered radically. The great landscape gardens that now feel 'natural' to us were not initially designed in any such spirit. Although the garden extended itself and opened out to the wider countryside, the idea was not to welcome in the natural but to extend civilization's control. The very term 'landscape

Below

Humphrey Repton was one of the first people to apply the word 'landscape' to the garden. This illustration of his Flower Garden, from Fragments on the Theory and Practice of Landscape Gardening *(1816), shows one of his more classically led designs.*

gardening' was not about natural topography but about Art.

'Landscape' itself is an entirely cultural term. When the word came into the English language, from Dutch, in the 17th century it was applied neither to the countryside nor to the garden. It did not describe the things that you see when you look out the window; it described a painting of what you see when you look out the window. It was a purely technical, artists' term to describe a particular sort of painting – a painting of the land as opposed to one of an individual (a portrait), or one of the sea (a seascape), or one of an event (occasional or narrative) and so on.

A century later the idea of a painting and the idea of the actual disposition and shape of the land

Above
This 18th-century view of Chiswick House Gardens shows the early influence of the Landscape Movement. The canvas is punctuated with idealized architectural features and an abundance of wildlife.

were brought together as a specific gardening term. Humphrey Repton (1752–1818) was an artistic young man pursuing various careers, and demonstrating good taste and a talent for sketching and watercolours. In 1788 he took up garden design with great seriousness and became immensely successful and fashionable. Jane Austen mentions him in *Mansfield Park*, making clear the esteem in which he was held: 'His terms are five guineas a day.' Partly because he was very hard working and partly because, unlike Brown or Kent his professional predecessors, he wrote books on the theory of gardening, Repton was enormously influential. He brought the expression 'landscape gardening' into use, explaining it thus:

> To improve the scenery of a country … is an ART which originated in England and has therefore been called English Gardening; yet as this expression is not sufficiently appropriate, especially since gardening, in its more confined sense of Horticulture, has likewise been brought to the greatest perfection in this country, I have adopted the term Landscape Gardening, as most proper, because the art can only be advanced and perfected by the united powers of the landscape painter and the practical gardener.[3]

Of course Repton, as he penned this, did not have any old landscape painter in mind – he was not thinking of the tidy foregrounds and fantasy backgrounds of medieval illuminations such as *Les Très Riches Heures du Duc de Berry*; nor of the 'simple' agricultural landscapes of Constable or later Van Gogh, and certainly not of the colour of bridge, water and lilies that Monet was to make one of the ideals of 20th-century gardening. He was thinking of neo-classical perfection – and particularly that expressed by the French artists Nicholas and Gaspard Poussin and Claude Lorrain; of those grand but tidy sweeps of grass, manufactured into vistas – long views with a clear focal point at the end of them, and above all scattered with classical figures, both architectural and human: the odd nymph, or great patroness disguised as nymph; the occasional pillar or temple, artfully placed – a nostalgic serenity, highly *human* – both in the sense of having human forms reposed about it, and in the sense of having artefacts (art, artefacts, artificial – never forget their close linguistic connection) which was of course entirely contemporary in its time.

Just how artificial and painterly Repton's approach was, can be seen in his Red Books: his beautifully illustrated morocco-bound design proposals for clients. In them he devised a system for showing his client's

present garden and its potential by lifting flaps on a picture of the original to reveal the proposed improvements, *in situ* as it were. But it was not just the horticultural elements that changed – uncivilized farm workers shown in the 'before' version were replaced by fashionable ladies promenading across the landscaped terrain of his proposed designs.

Influenced by these ideals, and by a fashion for them which had been building up – at Chiswick, at Kedleston, at Stowe and above all at Stourhead – rich landowners went out and made their own spaces into copies of such pictures. Alexander Pope, self-appointed public arbiter, claimed in 1734 that 'all gardening is landscape painting',[4] and Henry Hoare wrote to a friend in 1762 that his newly laid out grounds at Stourhead would be 'a charming Gaspar[d] Picture'.[5] The ideal was to make your widest view look like a landscape painting in the style of Poussin or Lorrain.

In the classical period gardens remained as cultural and as intellectual as ever. It is important to remember that Alexander Pope had a garden as overtly contrived as anything Bacon would have proposed – with an underground tunnel or grotto to reach the garden from the house. Although this grotto, which Pope regarded as something between a passageway and a reception room, was redesigned several times, the final version was decorated to resemble a mine in the West Country: geology, including fossils, and references to the mining industry were considered suitable devices for a garden even at the height of the 18th-century classicism.

Above

Successive developments in the garden at Stowe, Buckinghamshire, led to an extravagant 'natural' landscape. The Palladian bridge is perhaps the most impressive of the many architectural elements in the garden.

22

Many 18th-century ideas of garden design were political. The move away from the geometrical symmetry of the parterre and towards the landscaped approach was in part a patriotic and democratic statement: design your garden so that it does not look like a tyrannical French one. The English gentleman is portrayed as being at home in the country rather than the court; his instincts are at one with his agricultural peasantry. Other points of reference were philosophical – the *ferme ornée* of Marie Antoinette reflected new Roman ideals of the good life lived away from court – and artistic – the landscapes of Poussin crammed with classical references and allusions. Sir Joshua Reynolds wrote that a garden ought to have the 'marks of art upon it ... a cultivated spot – that it is inhabited, that everything is in order, convenient and comfortable; *which a state of nature will not produce*.'[16]

And throughout this period the idea of extravagant and elaborate jokes still cropped up: faked perspectives, preposterous follies, *trompe-l'oeil* and pretend hermits. The lake at Buckinghamshire's West Wycombe Park in the mid-18th century was designed using carefully positioned streams and plantings to represent a naked woman (later it was altered for modesty's sake to the shape of a swan). At Painshill in Surrey, in his self-consciously rococo garden, Charles Hamilton made serious, though unsuccessful, efforts to employ a real hermit to live in the fake Gothic hermitage he built in 1750. At Woburn Abbey in Bedfordshire, Southcote built a hen house with Gothic ornamentation and designed a vista which 'by distancing you may make an object look three times as far off as it is. This is done by narrowing the plantation gradually on each side almost to a point.' In Ireland Lord Orrery built a 'bone house' that was quite literally made out of animal remains.

There were more extreme examples. We like to think of Sir William Chambers as a colleague and a precursor to this very book. In 1772 he published his *Dissertation on Oriental Gardening* in which he criticized his contemporaries' garden designs. While recognizing that they were 'purer', simpler and less artificial and cluttered with detail than his own ideal, he saw this approach as leading too often to gardens that were unimaginative if not actually boring. He had already gained a somewhat mixed reputation for the exotic, bogus-oriental buildings he had designed for Kew Gardens – his pagoda, built in 1761, is still there. Now, in his dissertation, he examined or rather invented a fantasy Chinese philosophy of gardening. In China, he declared, three styles of gardening were recognized: 'the pleasing, the horrid and the surprising'. Later he also used the terms 'terrible' and 'enchanted' as alternative names for the last two types. He wanted gardens of high drama:

> The trees are ill formed ... seemingly torn to pieces by the violence of tempests ... the buildings are in ruins or half-consumed by fire. Bats owls vultures and every bird of prey flutters in the groves ... half-famished animals wander ... gibbets, crosses, wheels and the whole apparatus of torture are seen from the roads ... on the summits of mountains [are concealed] foundries ... which send forth large volumes of flame and continued columns of thick smoke ... from time to time. The [visitor] is surprised with repeated shocks of electrical impulse, with showers of artificial rain or sudden violent gusts of wind, and instantaneous explosions of fire.

The sinophile will realize that there are no volcanoes in China and as a point of fact Chambers had only visited a few sea ports there. This was an

Below
Hermitages, such as this example from Painswick in Gloucestershire, became very popular during the rococo period. The Gothic style was, and still can be, employed to great effect.

idealization – a creative concept. It was not taken up extensively by gardeners in Britain (although a garden volcano was constructed in Germany, near Dessau, in the 1790s), but it is possible to see the cascade and terraces of Corby Castle in Cumbria, or the clifftop faked ruins of the gardens at Hawkstone Park in Shropshire, within this rather extreme version of an old idea.

Even into the 19th century – as gardens became smaller, more domesticated and above all prettier, more floral – gardens (or more often bits of garden) in the Bacon tradition were still made. The 15th and 16th Earls of Shrewsbury laid out a garden at Alton Towers in Staffordshire in the late 1820s which included a replica of Stonehenge, a Swiss Cottage and, according to Loudon,

> such a labyrinth of terraces, curious architectural walls, trellis-work arbours, vases, statues, stairs, pavements, gravel and grass walks, ornamental buildings, bridges, porticoes, temples, pagodas, gates, iron railings, parterres, jets, ponds, streams … rock work, shell work, root work … entire dead trees etc., that it is utterly impossible for words to give any idea of the effect.[7]

But, on the whole, gardeners had lost that sense of their gardens as private and personal canvases on which their owners could mark out their own vision of the world for their solitary pleasures or social intercourse. The idea that gardens could make subtle and witty references to the world outside was gradually replaced with the idea that gardens were places of refuge *from* the world; they were not so much studies or hermitages for mental and spiritual work, but rather nurseries where gardeners could retreat from demanding effort.

Although concepts of the garden narrowed and lost their focus as a model or representation of the social condition – that is they ceased to be Art – the craft skills of horticulture developed enthusiastically. Gardeners got better and better at growing plants, even as they lost any strong sense of what they were growing them for. On the whole, gardens became increasingly organized around principles of decorum and propriety rather than being centres for the sort of philosophic and intellectual delight that Bacon had been thinking of.

By now the attentive reader will perhaps have noticed this highly selective history has almost entirely omitted flowers. It is true that Thomas Bushell, whose description of his own garden opened this chapter, omitted them too, but Bacon did not. On the contrary, flowers were a factor of the greatest importance in his dream of how gardens should be. In *Of Gardens*, before he turned his attention to design, let alone to wilderness mounds and the management of water, he wrote, 'I do hold it, there ought to be gardens for all the months of the year in which severally, things of beauty may then be in season,' and he struggled through the calendar trying to make practical suggestions for each and every season. His idea was to create within the garden a *Ver perpetuum*: an everlasting spring. Every bit as important to Bacon as his clear pools and geometrical layouts was his idea that a garden should produce blooms, fruits, foliage and perfume that would offer a display throughout the year.

Bacon had an immense scientific curiosity. During his enforced retirement he found consolation in working on the *Instauratio Magna* (the Great Restoration), which he hoped would supersede Aristotle's work as the foundation stone of a philosophical education. The reason for his desire to demote Aristotle was that Bacon believed the ancient Greek's whole method of deductive reasoning (from abstraction and authority to the particular) was impeding contemporary scientific research. Bacon wanted to argue from the particular to the general, and to do so with the greatest possible respect for the accumulation of data. His commitment to this project was considerable. In fact he died as a result of a scientific experiment: he caught a terminal chill while attempting, using a dead duck in a snow storm, to ascertain the precise effect of cold in preventing decay.

In his longer gardening work, *Sylva sylvarum*, Bacon reported in detail his observations and experiments on how to retard and advance flowering and fruiting; on how to germinate and propagate seeds; on how much water different species required; on fertilization and on many other aspects of the garden. Certainly at Twickenham and at Gorhambury he worked on developing this aspect of his gardens along with his finely paved streams, his witty topiary and aviaries, his artificial mounds and classical allusions.

Perhaps even more interestingly, when Bacon wrote *New Atlantis*, his unfinished Utopian fantasy, he provided no visual descriptions of gardens at all, but instead one of the 'fathers of Solomon's House', the governing body of the perfect Island of Bensalem, describes to the author the horticultural research that is continually undertaken there:

> We have large and various orchards and gardens wherein we do not so much respect beauty as variety of ground and soil.... In these we practice likewise all conclusions of grafting and inoculating.... And we make by art ... trees and flowers to come earlier or later than their seasons, and to come up and bear more speedily. We make them also by art greater much than their nature, and their fruit greater and sweeter and of differing taste, smell, colour and figure, from their nature.

Above

William Chambers' pagoda of 1761 still exists at Kew Gardens, standing as a reminder of the contemporary fashion for all things oriental. Although highly idealized, the use of foreign ideas showed great sophistication.

It would be fair then to argue that Bacon was at least as much concerned with horticultural progress as he was with design. This, consciously or unconsciously, is probably the one part of Bacon's gardening concept that is most familiar to us at the start of the 21st century. So familiar perhaps that it is difficult to realize just how 'magical', how extraordinary, ambitious and unnatural, this project of the *Ver perpetuum* was and how smoothly such ideas slotted into his overall understanding of gardens as being set against nature; as symbols of human civilization and control.

Despite having a considerable range of soils and eco-systems and, for its latitude, a very temperate climate, since its separation from continental Europe and the last Ice Age Britain's range of native species of trees and flowers has been severely limited. Most of our native flowering plants are small and with a short blooming season. The majority of our garden plants are either imported or hybridized – and in many cases both. When Bacon suggested a continuously flowering garden he was speaking at the dawn of both these processes; he was therefore looking outwards from his garden at two of the themes that intellectually engaged him most (and to which so much of his work was directed): European culture and contemporary science. When it came to flowering plants he was looking at 'novelties' not much different from hydraulic engineering, and mechanized automata. A garden that had flowers all year was one that specifically and explicitly spoke to the capabilities of human beings, their art and scientific skill.

Above

The concept of an eternal spring, so dear to Bacon's heart and so magically captured in Botticelli's Primavera *(c. 1478), has almost been achieved. But in the desire to attain year-round colour, many of the other intentions of Renaissance gardeners have been neglected.*

Moreover, of the 25 or so known botanical introductions in the century up to the publication of *Of Gardens* nearly half came from the New World, the Americas; or from China, Persia or Turkey, also new in the sense that they had been recently opened up to Europeans, mainly thanks to the increasing understandings of geography and the increasing skill of navigators – two important scientific concerns of Bacon's time. These plants were in themselves a symbol of adventure, human courage and burgeoning knowledge and skill.

This influx of imports continued unabated right in to the 20th century.[8] A garden plant as 'English' and ubiquitous as the common forsythia, for instance, was not grown in Britain until the mid-19th century. In the meantime cross-breeding and, eventually, a growing understanding of genetics was increasing the range of colours and the length of flowering of native and naturalized species. Compare, for example, the sweetbrier (the eglantine) which was available to Bacon with the long flowering multi-coloured roses available today.

Science went hand-in-hand with horticulture, and both with the human endeavour of the conquest of nature. The intrepid plant collectors of the 19th century would, we think, have delighted Bacon – and the plants that they brought home from far-flung expeditions would have aroused his enthusiasm and indeed horticultural skill. It is pleasant to imagine his delight in the invention of the Wardian case. From careful observations of his own ferns Dr Nathanial Ward became aware that plants could survive better in their own sealed environment. In the 1830s he sent some specially designed cases to Australia and in 1834 he received the first shipment of plants packed in their new cases. Dr Ward recorded their arrival with real excitement: 'I shall not forget the delight … at the beautiful appearance of the fronds of *Gleichenia microphylla*, a plant never before introduced alive into this country.'[9]

The Wardian case, invented using Bacon's own scientific method, took British gardening a major step nearer to Bacon's dream of the *Ver perpetuum*; it meant that many tender plants could at last survive the long sea journeys back to Europe.

Today, Bacon's everlasting spring has been achieved. Neither of us germinate in our gardens and we have no greenhouse or other winter protection, but there is always something in flower there, without our even thinking about it. It requires no particular skill or art on our part. We could just visit any one of the flourishing garden centres in our regions, pick up something in flower and stick it in the ground if we wanted to. To have flowers in a garden, even extravagant flowers in the dead of winter, is simply no challenge. After four centuries, the battle to manage nature in that particular way has been won. It is time to move on.

Bacon summarized his own life, probably quite accurately, by writing that he was not a great original thinker, but that his writing 'rang the bell that called the wits together'. Sadly few of the wits of gardening now respond to his calls. The modern re-configured, indeed transformed, understandings (and we would argue mis-understandings) of 'nature' and 'the natural' seem to have run their course. We have failed even to notice that we have won Bacon's battle; and we remain obsessed with blooms, with colour and with a pseudo-naturalism that too often has neither elegance nor wit.

As an alternative, this book returns to Bacon's idea of the garden as a part of human life: an artificial, constructed place for pleasures of various kinds that – as much as our clothes, our houses and our paintings – should tell people who we are, and help them and us to enjoy life. It is about garden wit, in both senses of that word – humour and intelligence. We are not interested in replicating Bacon's garden; there is very little here about reconstruction of any kind. Rather, we are interested in gardening in his spirit, using all the things that he would envy us for having, including plastics, electricity and modern plants.

Carving the
Landscape

Landscape is what happens when culture meets nature.

Simon Schama, *Landscape and Memory* (1995)

ANCIENT CHINESE THEOLOGY taught that the hills were the bones of the earth and, at the same time and inextricably entwined, they were also land dragons, sleeping under the blanket of soil. Mountains, hills and valleys, the 'landscape' was a living thing, vital and involved in the works of humanity – and especially in the work of making gardens. A garden had to call upon the landscape around it and under it, for without its aid the garden could not be successful. The pre-existing dragons were not hostile to the labours of the gardener, but they had to be treated with respect, honoured in the garden's design and its execution. Chinese gardens are famous now for the way they relate to their landscape, inviting distant features to participate in the overall effect, meaning and atmosphere of the garden.

This idea is worth brooding upon. In our urbanized culture it is easy to forget the ways in which the landscape, in both its largest and smallest manifestations, shapes our lives and forms the atmosphere of place that is so vital in the making of gardens. Every time we decide that we are secure enough to indulge in the pure luxury of gardening we are imposing upon the landscape, making it, changing it, developing it or destroying it. We need to strengthen our understanding of this rather crude fact because it is the starting point of all gardens, and without some consciousness of this we are unlikely to create satisfactory gardens. But we are talking about an active intelligent engagement, not a passive sentimental one: as we have already suggested, the word 'landscape' and the natural do not have much to do with each other.

Peter Osborne has made a garden at Clearbeck in the hills above Lancaster under circumstances that might break a man's heart. A vicious wind tears in from the Irish Sea, it has proved nearly (but not quite) impossible to find a place that is both sunny and sheltered, and the sloping site is both exposed and very wet. He does not seem discouraged, however, and has created one of the most personal and individual gardens we have seen, which none the less feels free of deliberate or provocative 'eccentricity': Clearbeck will come up in several contexts in this book. Peter Osborne is a birdwatcher, artist, Anglican lay-reader and mountaineer, and his garden directly reflects many of these interests. It is designed to make wild birds welcome – last year he had curlews nesting on an island in his small artificial lake and 47 other species

In the West, contemporary reinterpretations of ancient land carvings have become increasingly popular. This dramatic, water-spouting gargoyle in the Swarovski Crystal Worlds, Austria, was designed by André Heller. Sculpted from the landscape, it conceals a series of interlocking chambers, three storeys in height and covering an area of 2000m².

were also noted; it is dotted with sculpture; he has a fascinating 'symbolic' garden – through a pyramid folly representing death you enter a tiny, sheltered and sunny courtyard garden planned throughout with Christian symbolism in both the artefacts and the plants; and he has a beech-hedge circle oriented so that the three stern mountain profiles of the peaks beyond the garden create a distant backdrop.

The house at Clearbeck is old and sits securely on a slope so steep that the flagged terrace outside the back door is also the roof to a series of store rooms underneath it. The garden looks as though it has been there for ever, just waiting for someone to come and develop its 'capabilities'. From no single point can you see much of the rest of the garden – everything is 'just around the corner', hidden in exuberant planting or by the curves of the land itself. However, from the terrace and from many other points you can see out of the garden, towards the hills behind or over the grazing land that surrounds the homestead. Clearbeck, with its stream and string of curvaceous pools feeding into the substantial lake at the bottom, with its strong ribs and bones that create walk ways, viewing points, and continual changes of level, seems to have been designed by a curiously aesthetic local nymph with a great interest in horticulture. But in fact Peter Osborne created the landscape and all its details himself, with a remarkable sensitivity to the wider scenery in which it is placed.

When he came to Clearbeck it was still a traditional small holding with a steep yard beneath the farmhouse levered into a fairly sheltered corner on the edge of a valley. The mountains beyond were there of course, and so was the ground, which was so wet that wherever he chose to dig he could have a 'natural' stream; but there was not much else. Peter Osborne describes his process of garden design as 'carving the landscape', as a sculptor carves smaller rocks and stones. It is probably not coincidental that he was an artist, a sculptor, before he started. He has made his garden as an artist works any medium: he did not plan it on paper, but dug it out and built it up. Michelangelo is supposed to have said that the job of the sculptor was to find the statue inside the marble; Peter Osborne seems to be finding the garden inside the land. He does not use hammer and chisel, but a JCB, with which he claims to follow the hidden contours of the ground. The upper ponds have a feature that makes them look both elegant and spontaneous: the slope above them is terraced to make two paths between the water and the main lawn. The spoil from these three sinuous ponds has been used to create a mound, which cuts off the view of the larger lake and the hills beyond from this point and makes this inner area of the garden feel secret and intimate. Peter Osborne's longer term plan, however, is to turn the mound (currently growing tangled and untended) into a hide that will allow visitors to watch the birds on the lake. Thus an object that blocks a view will also become one to give a very specific and special view. The spoil from the big lake at the bottom of the garden has been piled up as a rampart on the farther side, containing the whole garden, allowing a long walk across what would otherwise be a bog, giving a raised place from which to observe the lake and its small islands, and reflecting the wider scenery.

<u>Right</u>

*The garden at Clearbeck
in Lancashire is complex
in its layout, with many
hidden and unexpected
corners. This straight
vista, however, cuts clearly
through the garden to the
landscape beyond.*

<u>Opposite</u>

*Due to the aspect and
design of Peter Osborne's
garden, many areas are
plunged into shade while
others bask in sunlight.
Glimpses of the ever-
present pools of water,
which connect each part
of the garden, reflect the
sky in their dark surfaces.*

Although the curves of the ponds and the slopes of the garden create a tender, enclosed feeling, Peter Osborne is not afraid of the straight line. From the terrace there is a very long perfectly straight alley, planted closely on each side and arched with an immensely high metal frame – a two-storey iron structure to support a rambling rose – so that one looks straight down a tunnel and out into the sunlight the other end. The vista is closed by a tiny arm of the lake and by a standing stone beyond the water. Beyond that again, the hills open out and the profile of the peaks is framed. From this narrow avenue, at least 90 metres (100 yards) long, other views present themselves: a second straight line, in this case formally framed in clipped beech, draws the eye across a classical circle, out of the garden and up to the crags in the distance. At a different point one's attention is directed more casually down towards the lake. More interesting, perhaps, than these traditional avenues is Peter Osborne's use of verticals: there is a point at which one can stand with the land sloping 'naturally' down towards the lake on one side, but on the other there is a straight drop, carefully walled, which gives a bird's-eye view of the vegetable garden. From the top it looks like a romantic sunken garden, but at the bottom one appears to be in a traditional walled vegetable garden. It is interesting how many of the gardens that feature in this book are artists' gardens – one of the reasons why the unexpected and often rather risky details at Clearbeck work so well is because they are created by a very skilled eye for balance, level, curve and contrast. But above all this garden is grounded in a sense of place, of the landscape in which it is located. When we went to photograph the garden, which Sara had visited once before, we got lost in the tiny lanes leading up to the area. We found the house, however, by the shapes of the hills around it. The garden – thanks to its gardener – has claimed the landscape, not by following what was originally there but by manipulating, managing and imposing new views, although always from a position of respect, if not love.

This is nothing new – although Clearbeck makes you newly conscious of it. Gardens have never really been a place to escape from the world, from culture and ideas and artistic sensibilities. On the contrary, they reflect and make conscious our ideas about the relationships between nature and culture; between the wild and the civilized. This has always been the case, whatever the vocabulary. It is not so much that *homo* is *sapiens*, that man is wise, as that we are a species that needs to meddle. Beyond use or practicality or necessity we need both to change what we see and to give it cultural meaning, to explain it, organize it and claim it as ours, as something human and important to us. We have always opposed culture to nature – and not just in the negative sense but in the positive sense as well – carving the landscape to give it symbolic and aesthetic meaning. Landscape *is* what happens when nature meets culture.

There is no such thing, at any scale, as a 'naturally beautiful landscape' – our perceptions of nature have been constructed by culture. One has only to note the differences thrown up throughout history. The differences between oriental and occidental ideas of the naturally beautiful, which lead to differences in what makes a good landscape. The differences between French, Italian and English gardens. The differences between 17th-, 18th-, 19th- and 20th-century English ideals of the perfect garden. And underneath these overarching shared ideals and social meanings there are the individual landscapes of the heart and mind.

We do not know exactly how the personality gains its individual tastes; psychoanalysis has some theories, but they never seem to explain very much about the strengths of likes and dislikes, of rightness and wrongness, of what pleases and what enchants. Such tastes must be acquired, as we acquire language, from the earliest memories of childhood, and yet it remains a mystery *why* a particular angle of light, a particular incline delights; why grazing cows in a field at the bottom of a garden are more satisfying to one person than sheep, while the opposite is true for the next person. Some people feel strongly that a garden must be enclosed, must be walled in like a cloister, while others are equally convinced that a garden should open out into the countryside and afford a wide view. Some people love the Fens – the huge

Opposite
Despite appearances, there are few natural landscapes remaining in the Western world. This part of the Napa Valley in California appears to be largely untouched, and yet it has been used by farmers for generations. More recently, it has become a popular tourist destination, well known for its nature trails and variety of snakes.

expanse of land and sky moves them emotionally – while others require hills and valleys to feel at home and to want to create a garden.

People usually come to garden design, to landscape making, as adults, with all these tastes in place, conscious or otherwise. Perhaps the primary job of great gardeners is to re-create that landscape of the heart, of their own dreams. That landscape will, of course, always be formed at least in part by social input, by culture, by what we might as well be honest about and call fashion, but our dream garden is never going to be the same as yours. In arguing for 'individuality' and even eccentricity, as we are going to do throughout this book, we are arguing for a way of saying 'this is MY garden. It is about me. I am its artist.'

A garden must express a point of view. This phrase has a double meaning. It has a simple physical sense: all landscapes and views must be observed from somewhere. Lateral vistas are a good example – half the point of them is that you cannot see them from point A, only from point B. How much 'surprise' or secrecy a garden should offer is a personal matter. Some people may want the whole garden laid open before them, totally visible from the windows of their bedroom. What this is saying is that they want a single point of view. Others desire something much more complex. For example, they want to lay out long vistas that will offer up a different view from each end. Some gardens offer surprising points of view, such as the unexpected opening up of a scene as a corner is turned. Where one is looking from affects what one is looking at. This is the point of view in its physical or technical sense.

But the observer creates the point of view as much as the object does. Great gardens always seem to be those that express the points of view of their makers. This is why, at their best, gardens can be considered Art. They express a unique voice, an individual vision, the views of a person who has brought certain experiences, sensibilities and skills (two of which are some self-knowledge and irony) to bear on the space available – who has indeed carved a landscape on to the land.

When it comes to making a garden, there are various approaches to fulfilling your dream. The first is the simplest, and the least practical. Choose your landscape. Do not start your garden, or even think about it, until you have found and acquired the landscape of your dreams to place it in. Look at art, study geography, travel widely and cultivate yourself. Learn which shapes, climate and degree of greenness, steepness and brightness, which quantity of trees, proximity to water and type of soil say 'Yes' to your probably unconscious yearnings. Then buy a plot in such a place and build a garden there.

Unfortunately there are a number of snags with this plan. One is that you may never find it, or not until you are too old to do anything about it; dreams are not realities, the place of your dreams may not exist, or not yet. A second is that most of us have to live where our garden is (this is presumably not absolute but it tends to be fairly determinant), which means that the garden has to be within range of the necessities imposed upon us by other parts of our lives – such as work, relatives and financial restrictions.

There is another reason why choosing your landscape fully and completely is unlikely to prove satisfactory: in as much as a garden is a work of art, you cannot know *exactly* how it will turn out until you work on it. Every writer or painter knows this – you have a general idea, a book or picture in the mind, but in the act of creation you change it. If this is true of all art forms, it is particularly true of gardens because they are fluid. What you put on a piece of paper or canvas tends to stay there – and although time, disasters and triumphs can change the artwork this is nearly always perceived as a loss, as a movement away from the original artistic intention. With a garden, however, the reverse is true – a new garden is a plan for a future garden. You certainly do not want it to stay exactly as it is; you will plan and even hope for future growth and development, change and decay.

Gardeners also change during this process. Some of the changes may simply be a growth in horticultural knowledge – one starts gardening and at some point one becomes a gardener. Working in the garden

Opposite

The owners of the Porter's Lodge in Suffolk created their fantasy garden in a magical landscape, drawing on the traditions of the Italian Renaissance. The fact that they have not erected a boundary fence enables illusion and reality to merge.

makes one interested in the garden; then one becomes interested in other people's gardens, one starts to look at them competitively, acquisitively, enviously or admiringly. One starts to read not only how-to-garden books, but also publications on famous gardens, on design, history and cultural reference points. One's historical knowledge deepens and one's range of possibilities increases. One starts to develop personal tastes and that affects what one reads next. All these things accumulate and inform the choices that one makes in one's own garden.

There are long odds against choosing the ideal landscape for your garden and finding that choice satisfactory throughout the garden's long development. It can be done – Craig Wincoll and Lionel Stirgess at the Porter's Lodge in Suffolk more or less managed it. Lionel Stirgess had some very strong ideas about the kind of garden he wanted based on an already formed historical knowledge – a passion for, and detailed understanding of, Italian Renaissance gardens – and a great deal of experience in design (this garden was to be made by a town planner and architect with real experience of the use of space and the meanings of architectural features). They deliberately sought out the place in which to make their garden. It is enclosed in a wood of extremely tall trees, which both frames the fabulous architectural and design details – of which more anon – and isolates the garden from the wider countryside, into which it would be hard to blend so extraordinary a garden. The house, which was previously the gate lodge to a mansion, forms part of the scenery. It is small, low and, like many old lodges, something of a fantasy building itself. The landscape means that when visitors arrive in the garden they are already in a dream state, just as by walking through the forest Hansel and Gretel enter a world of fantasy and discover the gingerbread house. Craig Wincoll and Lionel Stirgess found their fantasy landscape and went to work on it, but they were fortunate: this dreamy set-up is a second home that does not need to be compromised by the requirements of their work, or of other parts of their lives.

Luckily there are other approaches. Garden designers have responded directly to certain landscapes. Whatever garden in whatever landscape they had dreamed of, they modify their dreams, or even reconstruct them entirely, in response to the reality of their wider scenery. One of the most obvious and successful, indeed sublime, examples of this approach is Thomas Church's sinuous swimming pool in El Novillero, Sonoma Valley in New Mexico, which hangs, indeed appears to hover, over an enormous valley. The curves of the swimming pool reflect or repeat in the foreground the curves and rhythms of the river in the valley below. It is impossible to imagine this swimming pool existing anywhere else. It is landscaping in the purest sense of the word – even though the backcloth is miles away and untouchable – because the pool does more than merely reflect the distant river, it makes you notice it, its curves and meanderings. In other words, the flatness and clean lines of the valley are given shape and meaning by the clean lines

of Church's construction. In responding to the view, Church has changed it by making us see it afresh. He has done, in a highly modern idiom – indeed the whole idea of a 'swimming pool' would have been strange to an 18th-century landscapist – much of what the Landscape Movement was advocating, but in a very different way. He has not uprooted the distant river and its sun-baked plain, but used the foreground (the bit he can dictate to) to make us see the distance from a particular point of view. He has made a landscape, and an entirely contemporary one at that.

On a completely different scale, it is impossible to see the bizarre success of Derek Jarman's Romney Marshes beach garden, which could so easily have cowered under the shadow of Dungeness nuclear power station, as anything other than an artist's response to an extraordinary natural situation. The project was fraught with disaster: people do not usually make gardens on open pebble beaches; they do not usually start with nothing but a weatherboard shack; they do not usually begin when they know they have a terminal illness; and they never come up with a garden like this one.

Prospect Cottage, its timbers black with pitch, stands on the shingle at Dungeness.... Now the sea has retreated leaving bands of shingle. You can see these clearly from the air; they fan out from the lighthouse at the tip of the Ness like contours on a map.... There are no walls or fences. My garden's boundaries are the horizon. In this desolate landscape the silence is broken only by the wind and the gulls squabbling round the fishermen bringing in the afternoon catch.

There is more sunlight here than anywhere else in Britain; this and the constant wind turn the shingle into a stony desert where only the toughest grasses take a hold – paving the way for sage-green sea kale, blue bugloss, red poppy, yellow sedum.... High above a lone hawk hovers, while far away on the blue horizon the tall medieval tower of Lydd church, the cathedral of the marshes, comes and goes in a heat haze.[10]

Above

From many angles this breathtaking series of reflective terraces blends with the ocean beyond. The infinity pools form a giant watery staircase, leading from the house to the clifftop.

36

Something in Jarman responded to something impossible and harsh and lovely; and the garden expresses that response in a way that was bound to be highly individual, eccentric even, but also brave, avant-garde, magical. Indeed Jarman's garden goes further than that: it imposes a meaning on the bleak land so strong that, if you drive along the open road that runs beside it and the shacks and cottages of his neighbours, you cannot fail to notice that other gardens are now tentatively imitating him, incorporating pierced stones, piled pebble cairns and flotsam and jetsam into their immediate surroundings. Jarman has *imposed* a point of view and interpretation and meaning on the landscape through his own garden.

At some level every gardener responds to the natural contours of their situation when they come to plan and construct their garden – even if it is a strong negative response to the gasworks or the next-door neighbours' children which leads them to grow hedges to keep out the view, and to enjoy the narrowest, most private landscape possible. British culture has thrown up an odd phenomenon: a higher proportion of Britons are town and city, as opposed to rural, dwellers than any other Europeans. Britons aspire to home ownership, and particularly house ownership. Although most of us live in towns, we have a higher percentage of people who want to live in the country. Our houses are closer together, but we are more committed to privacy. Compare a British urban terrace with an American suburb: our houses are huddled closer together but are far more cut off from each other; not to be able to see your neighbours' garden is considered an advantage worth obtaining even if it cuts off all distant perspectives. (It is quite odd, therefore, that we don't have more roof gardens, which would seem to combine the best of both worlds. Perhaps these feel too 'modern' – despite their Babylonian origins – in relation to our rural dream, which tends to be towards the antique and the quaint.) Garden landscapes seem to be governed by an interior conviction that a 'proper home', and particularly a 'proper garden', is located in the midst of a country estate – a distant humble cot would be acceptable, but any visual sign of a neighbour would not. This theory would explain why, on the whole, front gardens – and we do have a lot of these – are so appallingly badly thought through, under-designed and dull. We do believe in landscape, but not in streetscape.

This is a shame because, as one can see in the Camley Street Nature Park in northwest London, a garden's atmosphere can be enhanced and enriched by an industrial urban landscape as well as a by a romantic rural one. Here the views of Regent's Canal have not been obscured by militant hedging or anything else and the longboats are part of the atmosphere. Even more importantly, one end of the garden is framed by the stunning red and black wrought iron filigree work of the King's Cross gasometers, which contrast with the organized wildness of the little park.

St Chad's Haggerston in Hackney, East London, has a Victorian Gothic vicarage, set in the middle of a post-war concrete council estate. It has a romantic walled garden behind it: part of the romance is in the planting, but part is unquestionably in the landscape. The garden is secluded on two sides by the façades of the church and the house itself, and has a well-planned and carefully developed aura of privacy, even secrecy. This is despite the fact that on one side of it, and barely 10 metres (11 yards) away, looms a hideous 17-storey block of council flats. The garden's sequential designers, both vicars, might have been able to hide the tower at the expense of most of the light, but its presence somehow makes the garden seem all

Above

Jarman's influence can increasingly be seen in coastal gardens around the world. The difficult conditions and reduced choice of plants in such areas can produce remarkable results. This example, from Pevensey Bay in Wales, shows a powerfully creative reaction to the challenges of the landscape.

the more sheltered, mysterious and unexpected, perhaps through some awareness of the grim outer world. Pretending it was in Gloucestershire – or any other rural setting – would have taken some of the magic away from a brave landscape and a garden made more wonderful by the contrast.

Most people consciously and unconsciously respond to the larger topography in the making of their gardens. Often it is to something simple – a slope, a curve, a mature copse, a single tree or (lucky gardeners) standing or moving natural water. If something is *there*, ready and waiting, and particularly if getting rid of it would be difficult, it influences the picture of the garden that we work through in our heads, as we think about making our landscape.

The garden writer Anne Wareham, whose own garden at Veddw House has been one of the bonuses of the researches for this book, has a particular and informed sensitivity to place: a kind of knowledge that is not only aesthetic, but also historical and topographical. Rather as Thomas Church did in northern Mexico, she has found ways of 'pulling the landscape into the garden'. This gives meaning and structure to her design, but also makes one look more carefully at the wider frame within which her garden sits.

The whole garden at Veddw is on a fairly steep slope, opening up views of the valley and mixed farm- and woodland rising on the opposite side, offering a landscape that is agricultural and mellow but with a fairly near horizon of curved and bumpy hills. The central axis of Anne Wareham's garden copies, on smaller scale, the larger scene: a valley runs down the garden, at right-angles to the big valley, leaving two facing slopes just like those in the larger scale landscape. She describes her strategy thus:

> I have covered a hillside with my tribute to our local landscape. The garden has a small valley. On one hillside, well situated for viewing from the opposite side, I have planted box-hedging, using the

Below
At Veddw House, Anne Wareham is creating her garden as a tribute to the local setting. She has planted hedges to reflect the shape of the field boundaries and the contours of the Welsh landscape.

pattern of field boundaries on the local Tithe Map. I am filling in the 'fields' that this makes with grasses and some hardy perennials, hoping to echo the appearance and subtle colours of the fields in the distance. It is, of course, an adaptation of a parterre. The box hedges are too small yet, and the whole thing is too newly planted to know how effective it will be, but I hope it will look good in winter as well as summer, with the fading flowers of the grasses framed in the pattern of the box hedges.... In our guide to the garden I have included some information about the history of the land and the people who worked and lived here, because I am fascinated by the traces of the past that I find, and I think some other people will be too. Cueing them into that theme may help them notice other signs of the land's history – the bilberries which are the remnants of the heath, or boundary banks and ditches.[11]

This is a very sophisticated approach to landscape; it acknowledges how much its history, including its previous owners, has shaped the land, and it honours that rather than trying to disguise it. It is a kind of thoughtful responsiveness which is, sadly, all too rare. Out of that response Anne Wareham is creating a garden (or part of her garden) that is both original and deeply embedded in its specific location, and in the whole history of gardening itself.

When one looks at the whole picture – the situation, the shape and the history of the land where a garden might be – it is important to include the house itself, as this will affect the orientation of the garden.

Above

Artists such as Andy Goldsworthy and Richard Long, whose 'natural' works give added meaning to the landscape, are sometimes outshone by the impact of age-old agricultural practices. These lavender fields punctuate the Provençal hills and cover them with a glorious purple haze.

In smaller gardens, especially, the house is likely to be the dominant feature of the garden landscape: for many of us it is the *view*, the landscape feature, of the whole of one side of the garden. Even in larger arenas the garden will be perceived, as Bacon realized, as an extension of the house. Only in parkland, or under rather unusual circumstances, will the house appear as a feature of the garden rather than vice versa. Moreover, it is far easier (and cheaper) to change a garden than to rebuild a house. In thinking about the landscaping of a garden it is crucial to take the house, its style and size and other features, into the fullest consideration; to respond to the house's style and placement as well as to the practical needs of the people who live in it.

Since 1989 Susan Cunliffe-Lister has been redeveloping the gardens of Burton Agnes Hall at Driffield in Humberside. The Hall is almost a fantasy version of a grand Elizabethan home, and its style dictated the surrounding landscape. Susan Cunliffe-Lister's response was that:

> I did not want to re-create an original Elizabethan garden but rather to combine the two Elizabethan ages – using some of the ideas of the first Elizabethans but incorporating them with new ones as well as the wide selection of plants and materials available today.[12]

The garden, which now includes a trellised knot garden and cloister, has picked up on the playfulness of the first Elizabethans by having colour-themed games gardens – giant boards not just for chess, but also for snakes and ladders, noughts and crosses, nine men's morris and hoopla. The 16th-century addiction to topiary has led to the development of ivy sculptures over frames, including a summerhouse and a long balustrade designed by Rupert Till to represent a chess set, with a king and queen, pairs of knights, bishops and castles, 37 pawns, five arches and a Cheshire Cat and White Rabbit. This whole elaborate arrangement, incorporating humour and fantasy, grew out of an informed response to a house that continues to dominate the garden, constantly appearing and disappearing behind the plantings.

In the past the 'landscape tradition' of English gardening went beyond simply responding to a given set of geographical circumstances. Part of the job of the gardener was to create a landscape. Although there is little else traditional in what Charles Jencks is doing in The Garden of Cosmic Speculation near Dumfries, he does have a sense of scale that seems more 18th than 21st century. He has created a brand new 12-hectare (30-acre) landscape into which to put his garden and express his 'new language' based on ideas drawn from chaos theory, molecular physics and the evolution of the universe. This carving of the landscape includes a 20-metre (65-foot) spiral mound and a 120-metre (394-foot) sinuous raised earthwork as well as newly constructed lakes. There is no 'natural' landscape in the world that looks like this, but it is landscaping – a huge and magnificent sculpting of earth and water – and only such a canvas could sustain the ideas and elaborations on the smaller scale that Charles Jencks is developing.

If you feel overwhelmed by the thought of what Capability Brown did on hundreds of acres, or what Charles Jencks is doing with tens of acres – or even what Peter Osborne is doing on less than five – it is worth bearing in mind that you can carve landscape on a tiny scale too. In fact we do it all the time – in altering the soil balance or isolating beds for ericaceous plants, we are changing the landscape. Certainly in digging out even the smallest pond or bringing in stone from elsewhere to make a rockery, we are creating landscape. When we throw up a fence, or plant a hedge, or cut a new gateway, we are creating landscape. When we plant a lawn where there wasn't one, or dig out a lawn and replace the turf with raked sand or gravel in the now fashionable 'Japanese style', we are making pictures, creating landscapes, directing what and how people see. There is little point in complaining that one's garden is too flat, for example, when there is little except cowardice to prevent one digging a pit and using the obtained soil to construct a hill, or even a few little mounds. We are free to landscape our gardens in a way that we are not free to

The intrusion of art and myth into a deciduous woodland claims this space as a garden in the landscape tradition.

pull down and reconstruct our houses: apart from needing to seek consent for chopping down non-fruiting trees with a trunk girth of more than 10 cm (4 inches) measured 1 metre (39 inches) above the ground, there are surprisingly few planning restrictions on garden design. While planning permission must be sought to place a porch over your front door, none is needed for most conservatories, summerhouses, earthworks, plantings, paths or other hard features. Too many of us lack a breadth of vision and an awareness of the falseness of landscape to claim and utilize it.

There is a final approach to landscaping, which is possibly the most useful to people who need to stay where they are and have small gardens. You can 'cheat'. At the Menagerie near Wellingborough in Northamptonshire (a garden wonderfully full of tricks and guile) a sense of space is provided by cutting different parts of the garden off from each other, laying out paths that make you walk an enormous distance to get not very far. Perhaps most craftily of all, in this context, both the summerhouses are in one style at the front – one is Gothic and one classical – and a completely different rustic style at the back, and each has two doors so that you can enter from and leave into totally different environments. It takes quite a lot of time and thought to realize that you have only seen two summerhouses, not four, as you proceed around the garden; and, as you never see more than one at a time, the sense of size is miraculously enhanced.

Japanese garden designers have a long tradition known as *Shakkei* – the art of 'borrowing' landscapes from beyond the gardens' real perimeters. Originally long views, particularly of mountains, structured the plans of the great country house gardens, such as those around Kyoto. As gardens grew smaller *Shakkei* increasingly came to refer to planning and planting schemes that screened out cityscapes and concentrated the eye on framed views of distant hills. This is a highly adaptable idea. Jill Billington in *Small Gardens with Style* describes designing a garden which happened to have a new housing estate being built behind it. She and the owners negotiated with the developers and got easy permission to plant trees beyond the garden fence. They selected some wild European Silver Birch (*Betula pendula*), which is reliable, tough and

needs no particular care. Then, within the boundaries, they planted a fancier birch (*Betula utilis* var. *jacquemontii*), which boasts the most dazzling white bark. The garden now appeared to end in a grove of birch trees, only three of which were actually in the garden.

On an even smaller scale, Sheila New, in the minute garden of her terraced house in Bridport, Dorset, has built what she describes as a 'borrowed vista', though some might think of it as a 'stolen' one. She constructed a path straight down the garden to a high wall at the end of it, then put a wrought iron gate in the wall. Behind her house are some allotments, and so through the picture frame of the gate she appears to have another garden waiting to be explored.

Throughout this book we will be looking in detail at examples of how to pull off such 'trickery'; at people who in many different ways have produced gardens that are individual, witty and express a point of view that is as unique as it is personal. But to be free to use one's imagination and intelligence to improve and broaden the appeal of one's own garden requires first of all a conviction that this is a legitimate way to proceed – that cheating is not cheating at all, but designing for delight.

The history of gardening is a history of manipulation, cheating, craft and guile as well as a history of growing horticultural knowledge, plant importation and improved botanical skills. The reality is that *every* garden is a landscape garden – it is a picture, a chosen and controlled work of art, even if the art is to make it look artless. Neither nettles nor ground elder, after all, are native to Britain – it is no more 'natural' to let them flourish than it is to build a tiny Silbury Hill or dig a pit of demons in your garden.

One of the things we want to urge in this book is that people become more aware of this crafty aspect of gardening – and that they make gardens that are trickier, wittier, bolder and more fun.

Opposite and Right

The Menagerie in Northamptonshire has only two summerhouses, but visitors who lose their sense of direction in this cleverly designed garden will think that there are four. Here, one of the summerhouses is shown from two sides – its rustic face (opposite) and its formal Gothic façade. The settings, too, appear enormously different, making the trick all the more effective.

Laughter like a Fountain

Nothing could be considered to have style which hasn't got such a commanding presence and elegance that it commands further examination. Or else a certain awkwardness which prevents it from being merely chichi. *And it would be bound to have wit: because you can't have style without lightness of touch and great exuberance.*

ELIZABETH TATE

IT IS MORE OR LESS IMPOSSIBLE to draw up a list of things that 'make people laugh'. Humour is far too individual for that. Here, Elizabeth Tate prescribes exuberance and lightness of touch.[13] We would want to add surprise, even shock, to that short list. Fear rapidly followed by relief, especially by the realization that it was rather silly to be afraid in the first place, is an infallible source of the giggles – just listen to any audience watching a Hammer Horror film. For centuries, people have been using spine-tingling effects to bring laughter to their gardens.

The best modern grotto in England, in our far from humble opinion, is in Roger Last's garden at Corpusty Mill in Norfolk. It was, like so many of the best garden features, conceived to solve a problem.

In one corner of the garden at Corpusty Mill nothing would grow properly, not even the boundary hedge that stood between the garden and the road. The corner was too dry and was totally shaded by a huge horse chestnut tree, which was not only very beautiful but also one of the very few existing features when the Last brothers started to garden there. There was a need to create a structure that would protect the privacy of the garden from the road (since the hedge was failing), that did not need plants and, moreover, that would positively profit from the shady nature of the place. They chose a grotto.

From the outside the grotto looks like a strange series of ancient mounds, or moss-covered domes, humped and irregular. Between them is an entrance: an arch beneath the moustaches of a high-relief face deliberately modelled on the grotto of the Sacro Bosco at Bomarzo in central Italy. This strange fantasy garden in central Italy is a sort of Renaissance theme park of the grotesque and fantastic.

Passing through the arch of the Corpusty Hill grotto, the explorer must descend some slightly scary steps in almost pitch darkness; but, curiously, once inside there is more light. This space is under the canopy of the horse chestnut, and its huge leaves filter the sunlight, giving it a strange greenish quality. In the first cavern of the grotto the hole at the apex of the dome is filled with a chunk of rock crystal, which further breaks up and refracts the light. There is a tiny fountain, a green ceramic snake coiled around a pot out of which water dribbles. The unfaced flint stones of the inner walls seem almost to move and dance in this

Opposite

Sadly, only one feature remains of the original garden at Pratolino – the statue of Appennino. Like the Lasts' ghost (see page 47), the carving inspires fright and shock, followed by laughter induced by its colossal scale.

44

Left
The grotto of the Sacro Bosco at Villa Orsini in Bomarzo, central Italy, provided the inspiration for the entrance to the grotto at Corpusty Mill in Norfolk, England. Witty ideas occur throughout the garden to surprise and delight the unsuspecting visitor.

broken light. The Lasts resisted, without too much difficulty, a standard lining of oyster shells here – theirs is more of a 'Gothic' sort of grotto than a classical one.

You move across the tiny enclosed space towards an apparently lighter archway, but it is a mirror that both refracts the light further and totally confuses the shapes, the size and the distance. This is disturbing, but eventually the visitor becomes aware that there are other tunnels, like a child's adventure story. There are several chambers set with ornamental bones and masks and including more openings above your head that spill green light. Then you turn a corner and there, leering at you, is a ghost. It is perfectly frightening, invoking that start of real though minor terror followed by laughter. It is, of course, a waxwork face swathed in a sheet.

Roger Last insists that the ghost was put in because this side of the grotto opens out, through a wrought iron grille, onto the village green, and they were worried about children breaking in. The domes above were not designed to be walked on, and a little element of fear might deter youthful vandals and thus keep them safe. Last claims that this has worked. But the real reason the ghost is here is to startle, because being startled is the right response to a dark grotto illuminated by green light. It is bold, risking bathos and accusations of kitsch, but it works perfectly. It is the moment of laughter that is all too rare in gardens nowadays, and that we need to recapture.

The heavy hand of sober good taste has fallen hard on contemporary gardens. We seem to have lost the light touch of wit, of humour and of what Bacon would have called 'conceits'.

As we have shown it was not always like this. When Queen Elizabeth visited the Earl of Leicester in 1575 he built a state-of-the-art garden for her, which included a delightful feature: 'water spurted upwards

Opposite Top
The waxwork ghost that greets you from the gloom at the exit to the Corpusty Mill grotto seems eerily real, especially as your senses are already confused by the darkness from which you are emerging. In this context it is perfectly terrifying – a leap of fear followed by laughter.

with such vehmency, as they should by and by be moystened from top to toe; the hees to sum laughing, but the shees to more sport.' It is too horribly easy to imagine what would happen today if one installed any such device in a garden so that earnest visitors were 'moystened from top to toe' while admiring a new gravel and grasses planting; or inspecting, baffled but willing, the species crocus or penstemon collection.

Leicester, it transpires, was quite restrained. His contemporary, Buontalenti, was building a garden for Francesco I de Medici at Pratolino that contained, among innumerable mechanical devices, a grotto where the host could, at the flick of a lever, so flood his guests that, to avoid drowning they had to flee up twisting staircases, while being drenched by hidden sprays (see page 18).

Even the neo-classical 18th century indulged its wit with faked perspectives, extravagant follies, *trompe-l'oeil* and pretend hermits. Right up to the Second World War a certain robust humour was still permissible: at Ladlew, in Maryland, USA, the topiary hunt – with mounted huntsman leaping a five-bar gate, hounds in full cry across the lawn and fox, tail held high, about to go to earth in a handy shrubbery – exquisitely clipped in yew, represents a continuity with that delightful tradition. And so, to a less grand scale, did some of the more satirical approaches to the carpet bedding that was ubiquitous in public parks between the wars: quite apart from the elaborate representations of trains, cars and animals, one summer Weston-super-Mare in Somerset presented a roll of carpet as a bedding feature.

These sorts of gardens all have an element of performance. This theatrical tradition of gardening has been more or less lost, which is tragic, especially as it seems to have disappeared at the very moment that we have available materials and technologies that

Right
The tongue-in-cheek humour and vitality of this topiary hunt at Ladlew in Maryland, USA, is sadly lacking in many of today's finest gardens and public spaces.

would have made designers such as Buontalenti weep with envy. We don't just have a range of plants unimaginable to any previous generation, we have plastics and polymers and resins. We have mechanical aids such as lawnmowers. Above all we have electricity. This, among other things, means that we can make the sorts of devices that Pratolino and other gardens of its period delighted in without being dependent on a steep natural drop for the hydraulic systems: we are no longer dependent on natural water pressure. We could do anything.

Take for example the motion-responsive switch. Imagine what Buontalenti could have done with it. This brilliant device, inexpensive and easily installed, could trigger infinite enchanting surprises in the contemporary garden, such as leaping fountains, exploding fireworks, smoking volcanoes and playing music. Yet we have only located a single, modest example of its use in a British garden: Jessica and Peter Duncan have a pond, beside which sits a large stone frog. Nearby movement causes the frog to spit suddenly – a jet of water that Peter Duncan originally wanted to spray the passer-by, but in sober reality splashes back into the pond. This does feel like an addition to the normal use of so ingenious a device – deterring burglars.

Though presumably Francesco I would have enjoyed that use as well – legend says that he and his mistress, Bianca Cappello, kept a pet leopard as their burglar deterrent. Bianca deliberately invited her estranged husband to Pratolino for a rendezvous so that the leopard could be set loose to attack him. (Whether or not this is true, it was not successful; the husband met a far more commonplace death –

Below

The oyster-shell-lined grotto at the Porter's Lodge is reminiscent of the Italian Renaissance, but possesses an entirely modern look and atmosphere. The lowest pond is crossed by formal 'stepping stones' and an iron seat appears to float on the surface of the water, surrounded by water lilies.

Above

Craig Wincoll and Lionel Stirgess commissioned and installed a working water organ for the Porter's Lodge. The only such organ in Europe, it is modelled on one that played at the Villa d'Este during the Renaissance.

stabbed to death by a moralistic relative of *his* mistress. Perhaps it is not altogether surprising that they went in for theatrical gardens.)

It is hard to find examples of this Italianate or theatrical wit in contemporary gardens. The Porter's Lodge – Craig Wincoll and Lionel Stirgess's Suffolk garden – is an honourable exception; perhaps because it was designed not by a gardener but by an architect and town planner, someone used to dealing with a constructed environment. On its own scale, this amazing garden has a lot in common with Italian Renaissance villa gardens: it is divided into 'rooms', but with many more interlinking views across and out of different areas, vistas, and a strong sense of direction, of moving through the garden. 'Growing up near Chatsworth' inspired a love of waterworks and these abound. At the simplest level they include a semicircular canal fed by a beautiful copper carp; a very simple architectural bubble fountain that makes no reference to 'nature' whatsoever; and a neatly framed 1-metre (3-foot) vertical squirt rising from a stone ball and falling into a circular pond. There is a larger darker pond behind a medieval gateway with a drawbridge and artificial ducks; and a stag standing above a water-wall that flows over a carved lead panel. But above all, and when the visitor is well prepared, there is an oyster shell–lined grotto in an entirely modern idiom, which none the less reminds one of the Villa Lante in miniature: water flows over the shells, catching and refracting light, and falls into a three-tiered pond. The lowest and largest of the levels is crossed by formal square stepping stones and in the middle there is an iron seat, which appears to be floating on the pond 'so that you can sit like a mogul emperor surrounded by cool water'. And next to it, in a tiny garden of its own, is a water organ. The only working model in Europe, it is based on the Renaissance one that played long ago at the Villa d'Este. Lionel Stirgess saw an exhibition model and is now having one built by Boggis Organs in Diss. It is important to stress that this is not an 'imitation' garden – it is not a copy or even a pastiche of an Italian Renaissance garden – it is a modern interpretation, a development of ideas about gardens that have sadly been allowed to fade from consciousness.

But such imaginative and energetic wit has become distinctly unfashionable, even frowned upon. Now, alas, Article 15 of the Royal Horticultural Society's directive for the Chelsea Flower Show *explicitly* forbids the exhibiting of garden gnomes: 'highly coloured figures, gnomes, fairies or any similar creatures, actual or mythical, for use as garden ornaments' are not allowed. We are grateful to James Bartholomew's extremely amusing and nastily accurate *Yew and Non-Yew: Gardening for Horticultural Climbers* for this information. Interestingly, when he tried to follow up the reasoning behind this curious regulation, he was fobbed off with some increasingly bizarre excuses, and finally an exasperated 'All right. We just don't like gnomes. We are snobs, so there.' Bartholomew was pursuing ideas of 'class' and 'taste' in gardening. Our concerns here are slightly other: we are more interested in the idea that you are not 'supposed' to have anything witty – even though 'tasteful' historicity is dangerously prevalent. You can exhibit 16th-century knots, classical divinities, wood nymphs, and naked maidens all you like; you can reproduce monastery gardens, 17th-century formal gardens, 18th-century pavilions and 19th-century herbaceous borders; you can pastiche tortured Japanese trees, Himalayan mountain plantings, alpine beds, and tropical island exotica – all of these are 'real' gardening. But gnomes are not allowed. We suspect this is because they are usually smiling.

This is a shame. Gnomes, after all, come from a noble tradition: they were introduced into Britain from Germany by Sir Charles Isham in the 1860s to adorn his rockery – a garden feature that developed from the German Romantic style. Goethe, *the* voice of the high Romantic Movement, praised painted garden gnomes for representing wild and magical nature – a view he thought was shared by many. A character in one of his poems reports that 'Every traveller stood and gazed thro' the rose coloured railings / At the figures of stone and the colour'd dwarfs I had placed there.'[14] (Note that he also found *pink* fencing a desirable garden feature.)

Moreover gnomes and their kinfolk were to be seen in many a traditional cottage garden, where the humble peasant mixed vegetables with cheerful annuals, herbs and perennials. This has now become a chic if ubiquitous gardening style that – minus gnomes – the Chelsea Flower Show has done a great deal to perpetuate and develop over the last decade. If historical authenticity was a serious concern, gnomes – together with thatched well-heads, painted stones and filigree fairies – would head the list of desirable garden features.

It is not, to be honest, that we want to fill our gardens, or have you fill yours, with gnomes, but it can be done well. Susanna Johnston, in her garden near Faringdon in northeast London, has a shameless and delightful gnomery, along with more expected wild meadow plantings and rather less usual arrangements of life-sized, gaudily painted fairground elephants and other zoo and circus figures. The effect is both bold and charming. She argues persuasively that rearranging the gnomes is a more attractive introduction to gardening for small children than weeding, but there is a child in every creative gardener who is too often suppressed. The children make a respectable excuse, but the gnomes really should not need one.

Above

The controversy that followed the inclusion of David Stevens' red rock in a garden for the Hampton Court Flower Show is a prime illustration of how we may take ourselves too seriously when thinking about gardens.

At the moment there is a distressing earnestness in gardening. Recently in a show garden Professor David Stevens, the eminent British garden designer, included some rocks that *were painted bright red* at the Hampton Court Flower Show. It caused widespread complaints. What logic dictates that it is acceptable to buy fake stone (whether from a non-local source or even reconstituted), place it in your garden and treat it with yoghurt to 'weather it', but that it is totally unacceptable to paint it? An entirely 21st-century logic of the *soi disant* 'natural' coupled with two deep fears, of being 'pretentious' and of being 'vulgar'; that's what.

This does seem sad. By tradition a garden is a 'pleasance', a place of pleasure, of amusement. It is the one part of a home that is entirely for delight. A garden's main function is to be enjoyable. Serenity is certainly enjoyable, and so, for some people, is the horticultural triumph of successfully growing new or difficult plants, or arranging them in themes and patterns. But so is laughter. It is key to social pleasure: a garden in which no one ever laughed would seem strangely inappropriate to most of us; so why does a garden that makes you laugh feel unacceptable?

All is not lost. There are flickers of inspiration widely scattered throughout the country; there are deeply witty, and even truly giggly, gardens. There are gardens that, from the shorter perspective, appear radically modern, but which in fact are keeping alive a tradition as old as ornamental gardening itself. In this chapter we are looking at good practice in this area. Before setting out, though, it is crucial to remember that with wit there can be no rules. What one person finds funny another finds silly, tasteless, inexplicable or mad.

<u>Right</u>
Margot Knox treads a fine line between the highly decorative and the kitsch in her Mosaic Garden in Melbourne, Australia. The sheer nerve, balanced with sensitivity, that engendered it, however, encourages others to explore their own ideas of what is 'good taste'.

George Carter, definitely a witty garden designer, thinks that truly witty gardens cannot be ordered from designers for this reason. Ask anyone cold to 'tell a good joke' and they will fall silent with embarrassment: wit and humour are highly personal and highly contextual. The best that this chapter can do is to encourage people to think of their own jokes to make in their own gardens out of their own circumstances, frames of reference and senses of humour.

Such gardens require sensitivity and thought and, perhaps above all, they need nerve. Margot Knox, the creator of the now famous Mosaic Garden in Melbourne, is well aware of the dangers, pointing out that 'the line between highly decorative and kitsch is very fine indeed'. And George Carter said much the same thing in a 1999 interview for *English Garden*: 'People may worry that what I do is rather *outré*, even vulgar, but the best schemes always sail close to the wind in terms of taste.'

So, let us return to Corpusty Mill, one of the finest gardens of this genre. It was designed and made by its owner, Roger Last, with his brother, John, who sadly died ten years ago. It is constructed within the yard of the old mill that had been their childhood home. It treads a delicate line between cutting-edge design and bad taste. Are the white hands flung up under the faux bridge in the small lake emerging (romantic) or drowning (macabre)? Is the folly a Gothic pastiche or children's dream castle? Is the face peering out of an arched medieval window silly or funny? Does the monkey puzzle tree in a more or less naturalistic park area give a hint of suburbia or of Stowe? Is a bust of the Emperor Hadrian (who built the great wall to keep out the Picts) inserted into a modern brick and flint wall, a deft classical reference or a bit of showing off? Is a direct 'quote' from Chatsworth – a 'soft' cascade a trickle down a rocky face – pretentious or workable in a 0.6-hectare (1½ -acre) garden? Is a two-dimensional painted statue of Vita

Above
Is the figure drowning or emerging? Touches such as this are typical of the atmosphere at Corpusty Mill in Norfolk, balancing as they do cutting-edge design and bad taste – all of them somewhat childlike in their humour.

Sackville-West peering in at the kitchen window from a tiny patch of shaded garden peculiar, boasting or teasing?

As is probably clear by now, we would personally defend the Lasts on every single one of these questions: the garden is unexpected, delightful, hilarious and deeply satisfying. The question is not Does it work? but Why does it work? One answer is that it is a garden that would be pretty wonderful without its 'eccentricities'; exquisitely arranged not, as Last describes it, 'in rooms, which suggests some sort of enclosure', but in sections, each hidden from the other by lavish planting. The planting itself is careful too: the skunk cabbage *Lysichitum americanus* is a fabulous water garden plant anyway – but until we saw it, beneath the 'Chatsworth' waterfall, splashed and bejewelled with water, almost translucent leaves of a giddy green through the wetness, we had not realized just how fabulous. Hydrangeas, especially the *arborescens*, do look right – however unexpected – in a 'wild' woodland planting. And an *H. petiolaris,* originally growing up a tree and now supported only by its dead stump so that it resembles a giant bush, is spectacular; the fact that the wood, which is actually very small, is entered through a medieval church archway is an addition to, not an excuse for, gardening. The grass around a pond, which is sunk directly into the lawn without any coping, is perfectly trimmed. Gardening decisions, such as edging the grass paths in the more formal areas exquisitely but letting them go 'soft' in wilder patches, have been made – the architectural elements are not meant to 'make' the garden, but to extend the pleasures it offers.

There is also something very acute about Last's sense of scale. At one corner a huge 'classical' face breaks through a wall looking with desperate surprise over a bridge, both suggesting something unexpected and

Below

A larger than life face looks out from the wall in which it is contained. It suggests something unexpected around the corner, and the incongruity draws you through the garden with a smile on your face.

inviting you to turn the corner. The image of someone larger than life walled up for ever is irresistible. Originally, Last had planned to have feet poking out of the bottom of the same wall, which would have added to the humour – but the wall was not high enough; it was impossible to make it look exactly right and so was firmly abandoned. Restraint within such an unrestrained atmosphere is probably as valuable as nerve in the end.

More importantly there is something completely unslavish about the imaginative impulse in this garden. We have said Gothic grotto, Roman statuary, medieval castle; we have mentioned Bomarzo, Chatsworth and Palladio; but these are inspirations, points of reference or departure rather than quotations, and they are used with intelligence and flair. Last is committed not to 'copying' but to creating a contemporary garden even if inside the Palladian dome is the 'only Tuscan tomb north of Italy' – a complicated *trompe-l'oeil* mural. This is evidenced in the happy use of contemporary materials: the trapped classical face in the wall, for example, is made of fibreglass. Roger Last is trying – despite some difficulties, partly brought on by the ignorance of the manufacturers – to research the longer term effects of water on aluminium, which he would like to use as a reflective backplate for a water feature in the winter garden he is currently creating. This mixture of pre-planning, using rather than copying, and on-the-spot, hands-on experimentation means there is nothing of pastiche in the garden: it is a personal garden and if part of a person is to be humorous, to be funny occasionally (or more than occasionally) at an intimate level, then this garden reflects something humane that is not seen often enough in contemporary horticulture and design.

There are of course other sorts of humour. Judy Wiseman, a professional artist, also has a wonderfully witty garden, one of the funniest we have seen. A small, square, rather dark space behind a conventional north London 'villa'-style house has been converted into something quirky, irreverent and teasing. In some ways this is less of a 'normal' garden with added decoration than a studio displaying an endless array of jokes. The largest, most obvious, of these is the nest: a straightforward wooden-platform 'tree-house' has had woven around it a bird's nest of withies so that it forms a gigantic brooding space above the garden. The garden is 'littered' with preposterous statuary: a neighbour with her curlers under her scarf leans over the garden fence chatting – it takes a second glance to see that she does not exist below her bust line and is hooked on to the garden boundary by her own elbows; a small boy climbs high up a tree trunk, managing the vertical in a style likely to give every careful mother a heart-stopping lurch; a naked woman bathes in the small pond, surrounded by floating balls from a toilet cistern. The size of the jokes continues downwards: in the flowerbeds resin toadstools grow alongside more vegetative plants, but life-sized noses and fingers also poke up through the cracks in paving stones, or are carefully clumped in the recommended horticultural 'groupings'. The flowerbeds are not divided from the paths by reclaimed Victorian pottery ropes or clipped box hedges, but by cast resin models of the owner's hands and feet, which charmingly imply all the work involved in maintaining a garden.

Much of this is completely original, and the objects themselves so unexpected that they presumably could not exist without Wiseman's artistic know-how; but some of her jokes are more referential (NOT

Above

Judy Wiseman's garden in London is full of laughter, caused by her turning the seemingly ordinary into the preposterous. Here, a perfectly normal pond has been transformed into an unexpected bath tub.

deferential). The current obsession with knot gardens and parterres is satirized twice in this tiny garden: once in a lavender triangle backed by two mirrors on either wall of a corner, thus appearing to present an absolutely symmetrical planted square; and once in a reclaimed old font in the centre of its own little enclosure – an elaborate knot garden less than 60 cm (2 feet) across made of box hedges barely three inches tall. Here satire and skill come together to create a feature that is truly enchanting.

In a novel by Margaret Drabble, one character asks tentatively, 'Do you think I've gone too far?' and another replies, 'Can you go too far in the right direction?' We would like to see more of this attitude in modern gardening: it is about boldness and following an instinct a little beyond where you would expect to stop; but it is also about 'lightening up', not taking yourself or your garden quite so seriously.

Or, at another level, more seriously. As Anne Wareham, the gardener and garden writer, points out, we are terribly earnest about flowers but shy away entirely from the more intellectual aspect of gardens. We no longer expect, or even want, a garden to make us think, to give us ideas; we just want to *look*, to be 'given' a garden directly to our physical senses, while leaving our intellectual capacities strictly alone:

> In the 18th century people deliberately set out to stimulate thought, with the idea that this would enhance the experience of parts of the garden by exaggerating a particular mood. A gloomy woodland part might have a statue reminding the visitor, through a shared knowledge of classical references, of the transitory nature of beauty and life. A sunlit garden full of roses might refer the visitor's thoughts to love and courtship by means of a cupid. Perhaps, elsewhere Bacchus might encourage thoughts of leaving for the nearest pub? Now we have not only lost most of this particular shared reference system, but any interest in having a garden stimulate thought.

In response to this set of ideas Anne Wareham has included in her garden a number of jokes about gardens. These are of a subtler, indeed in the 17th-century sense of the word 'wittier', kind than the artistic, visual jokes of Judy Wiseman. Anne Wareham is very concerned with exposing some of the confusions of our current ideas about what is 'natural' or 'wild'. So she plants tulips in her 'wild flower meadow', mentioning – and we suspect this is key – that 'large daffs of the public roundabout type would have made the thinking point just as well as the tulips, but I'm only prepared to play these games if they add to the pleasure of looking at the garden'. Elsewhere she has a 'natural' planting of bluebells, buttercups and poppies – the traditional flowers of the countryside – but instead of using field poppies she has used *oriental* ones. At the aesthetic level it works very well, with the same glowing primary colours, but it is a lovely humorous reminder that 'natural' is not natural; that mowing and weeding and care and knowledge are needed to get this relaxed result. To make the point Anne Wareham also has a formal garden: a proper 'room' enclosed by clipped yew hedges, laid brick paths and six rigorously rectangular brick-edged raised beds in which she grows massed 'wild flowers' – the traditional field flowers, blue cornflowers and field poppies – cavorting as 'garden' species.

Wareham manages her area of woodland in the same spirit. It is carefully designed not to look as a woodland 'used to look' when it was coppiced or had animals grazing through it. 'It looks like most of us *think* woods used to look. Making things look natural is a vastly underrated skill.' And then, in the depths of this pretend natural environment, Wareham pulls the plug on you – attached to some of the trees are little enamel plaques with poems on them; a 1-metre (3-foot) long lizard made of enamel discs like scales crawls up a tree; and in a glade in the magic forest a television set sits on a tree stump inviting viewers.

You have to 'be in the know' to get these complex jokes, but there is nothing wrong with 'in jokes' (provided their humour is not predicated on the idea that other people's ignorance is in itself funny), especially at the moment when so many of us have had our intellectual sensibility dumbed down by a

Below

This seemingly 'natural' wood in Anne Wareham's garden at Veddw contains many 'unnatural' items, echoing an 18th-century tradition of stimulating thought. Here, a lizard made of scale-like ceramic discs crawls up a tree.

55

century of debate about the natural versus the formal, conducted as though there was a simple and unambiguous distinction.

The television in the woodland is a very simple joke: it is the humour of incongruity which is, and always has been, a potential source of laughter. Moreover, it has the marked advantage of being relatively cheap to introduce into the garden – while many of the best garden jokes require either considerable artistic and creative skill or a substantial financial outlay, placing a broken television in a wood requires little effort or money. But even when the chosen objects are not free or almost free, they still require little design or hard landscaping commitment. You get a great deal of effect for your outlay. The effect is so simple – or seems to be, there are snags – that it is quite remarkable that this device is not used more often. A moment of incongruity not only makes people smile, but also makes them look at the garden afresh, makes them see better. Anne Wareham tells a rather interesting story about a small child in her woodland who discerned in the plaques and ornaments clues to a treasure hunt, or trail, although none had been intended – his eyes alerted, he started to look at the whole garden in a new way, noticing details in perfectly

Below

Incongruity can effectively transform the mundane into the amusing or witty. In this small town garden, designed by Cleve West and Johnny Woodford, everyday objects are given a new edge with the clever use of juxtaposition and colour: orange augers are mulched with iron chains and backed by wooden balls.

natural plants and structures that he would never have seen without the original artifice. The incongruity of enamel plaques in woods, of television sets in glades, woke up his mind and with it his eyes to the 'natural' environment in an entirely fresh manner.

There are also the shocking and amusing incongruities of colour. We have become so narrowly conservative in our gardening imagination that something painted almost any colour except black, white and dark green creates a sense of incongruity. Painted walls, furniture and even, as David Stevens demonstrated, rocks can create a frisson of laughter by their very improbability. Johnny Woodford's bright orange garden in Brighton takes this very basic idea into a new dimension – all his work with Cleve West constantly asks where the line between gardens and other art forms really falls, but his own garden makes the point very simply. If we are happy to hybridize and plant for colour effect, why do we hesitate over paint? Goethe's rose-pink fence and Woodford's burnt orange walls suggest that there is no real reason not to go for bright colour schemes in hard features as boldly as we do with plantings.

It sounds very simple. Take any old 'unnatural' object, plonk it in your garden and watch visitors crease themselves with laughter. In practice there do seem to be rules. The first is that this particular sort of humour works best where the garden is, at least at the superficial level, quite traditional in terms of planting. Corpusty Mill has been described as a 'picture postcard dream contrived to welcome and reassure visitors while at the same time soothing and quieting their perception so that they will be even more astonished, shocked and delighted by the hidden sections of the garden.' This captures precisely the technique of incongruity – it has to be unexpected.

Above

Johnny Woodford's own garden plays with scale and materials to stunning effect. Iron and wood candle holders rest against a steel wall; an enormous keyhole punctuates a bulging door; a lawn forms a roof over the entrance. These features may seem straightforward, but the effect is easily overdone, at which point the wit disappears.

For much the same reason, the joke has to be 'hidden' so that it can be stumbled upon unexpectedly. This means that such trickery cannot be repeated too often. It is tempting once you have started thinking in this way to cram the garden with the unexpected, the incongruous, the *objet trouvé*, but beware of overplaying your hand – after being shocked a couple of times, the visitor will cease to be surprised and will begin to look for the jokes rather than being startled by them. They will become congruous and thus lose their original point. If you knew in advance you were going to 'by and by be moystened from top to toe', mentally if not physically, you would simply avoid the whole experience. Some gardens, such as Judy Wiseman's, Derek Jarman's or Margot Knox's fabulous mosaic garden, might seem to disprove this theory, but they are offering the whole garden as a single incongruity; their work is incongruous to our ideas of what a garden is meant to be like, rather than containing a series of incongruous effects within a more standard garden.

One of the strange things about gardens is that people enjoy the experience of being tricked, deluded and even confused in them. Elsewhere, even inside the home, people tend to feel irritated and conned if their sight or other senses deceives them. If you made the inside of your house look like Versailles by the use of mirrors, fake façades, unnecessary corridors that meant you had to walk 100 metres (109 yards) from sitting room to kitchen, people would find the experience irritating and consider you pretentious.

Do the same thing in your garden, however, and visitors will be amused and delighted. If you lay out your plan so that people think you have several acres that take an hour and a half to walk round when in fact you have a flat plot less than 46 metres (50 yards) long, if you convert your garden shed into a Doric temple, paint a long view on to your red brick boundary wall, or create an arch in your hedge that invites exploration but in fact leads only to the compost heap, your visitors tend to be enchanted. Perhaps somewhere in the inner recesses of our subconscious we all know that *really* a garden itself is an artificial construct; that it is never a natural object, but always a work of art. We know that the silver birch grove with its dazzling white bark is not 'natural' to the hillside it adorns, but a loving fake – *Betula utilis* var. *jacquemontii* – imported from the Himalayas. We know that the native English rose flowers but for a day, is savagely prickly and will rampage through a garden destroying everything in its path. That the charming rambler that adorns many a garden with its sweet-scented double flowers is a carefully bred treasure that is pruned, given props, fed, looped, tied and entwined with the greatest possible artifice. We may hide this knowledge because we yearn for the 'natural', but in the end we get great satisfaction from being deceived and then being allowed to admit it.

This is not the whole story, however, because only certain sorts of deception satisfy – we have never heard of anyone being thrilled to discover that the glorious roses they have just admired are actually plastic. A lawn studded with obviously 'fake' wooden tulips did attract attention at Chelsea in 1999, but there was no attempt to deceive. The same thing could be said of Mary Doogan's trees, which were constructed entirely from dead wood and string. In 1999, the Jack in the Bush garden-art gallery near Hull displayed some exquisite ceramic flowers staked into a border. And there is no doubt that Judy Wiseman's resin fungi are very effective. There does seem to be a subtle division between 'imitation' and 'art'.

So illusion in the garden does please. It pleases twice if it is done well – once in the amusement of discovering you have been tricked and then, retrospectively, it draws attention to the pleasure of what you thought you saw.

As we have already shown, the idea of making your garden look 'bigger' by constructing false perspectives, especially along vistas, was considered an art form in the 18th century. As the average garden is smaller now than in the past, the need for this art and the difficulties of constructing it have got greater. The false perspective is currently the most practised garden illusion; sometimes it is executed on the two horizontal planes simply by paths and plantings that imply the garden is infinitely more spacious than it is.

Nan McAvoy's garden in Washington D.C. is an fine example of a design where a great many of the classical tricks of perspective have been used to modern effect. The garden is small – 15 x 9 metres (50 x 30 feet) – and hemmed in by neighbours. The owner wanted a timeless classical feel, raised beds for easy maintenance, a home for a favourite statue and a swimming pool. She obtained them all. The swimming pool is neither long nor deep – the length of the garden constraining the former and the unfortunate presence of drains and cables barely 1.2 metres (4 feet) under ground preventing the more usual 'deep end'. But it is made to look deeper by lining it in black and by using shiny black tiles rather than more usual pool colours. It is made to look longer by using two specific devices: a visual one and a cultural one. The pool is not actually rectilinear, the sides converge, drawing the eye towards an implied distance, just as a painter creates perspective. Also, by placing an entirely fake classical portico with its niched statue at the far end of the pool, the designer not only provides a hidden place for the swimming pool's necessary machinery, but also refers the viewer to the 'canal' of 17th-century formal gardens. Canals are narrow, smooth, reflective, *long* reaches of water with pavilions or porticos at the far end. By having all the other requirements, the design manages to suggest the missing one – length.

This garden contains a number of other devices of great ingenuity. Behind the swimming pool the purity of the mood is threatened by a particularly ugly industrial wall on the right, but enhanced by a dogwood on the left, which was in fact already growing in the neighbouring plot. A satisfying, though false, symmetry has been created by placing a matching dogwood behind the screen, which appears to match the pre-existing one although they are in fact in different gardens. This distracts from the forbidding wall and prevents it from dominating the scene. A crafty flight of steps leads down from the house to the garden. The risers and the edge of the flats are constructed of white stone, but the width of the horizontals are grassed to match the lawn below, making the steps look far wider than they actually are. Thus the garden pleases as a scene while offering an additional grin of appreciation once the enormous guile has been uncovered.

In his Oxfordshire garden the photographer Andrew Lawson has created a miniature version of the same 'trick'. Starting with what he himself described as a very boring square, Lawson's first intention was simply to break it up in various ways, and distort its rectilineality. As well as having the smallest imaginable pleached alley, Lawson has what he jokingly calls the 'only sea view in Oxfordshire.' First he constructed by means of trellises a division of the far half of the garden. One quarter is now a vegetable and herb garden that includes a ziggurat, which serves both as a mound, to give an elevated point to the flat garden, and as a planting area and display space for his wife's statuary. In the remaining quarter, not more than 15 metres (16 yards) long, he constructed a vista – basically a narrowing lawned path that leads to a wall. In the wall a recess has been built, on the back of which he has painted a seascape, or rather a bit of seascape, as though seen through a hole or window. Again this adapts for modern circumstances the old *oeil-de-boeuf*: the hole cut in a hedge or wall to bring more distant prospects within the sphere of the garden. The narrowing of the path, the artificial perspective, does make the view feel longer, but to emphasize the effect Lawson has designed the trellis, which backs the flower borders each side of the path, so as to reflect the same trick: the distance between the parallels of the trellis (both vertical and horizontal) also narrows and brings them closer together. This trellis is fairly heavily planted, so the effect is partially hidden. When we visited him, Lawson wondered if it had been worth the effort; but it certainly was – a lack of attention to detail is always obvious in such effects. The South Walk at Sutton Place in Surrey has been cunningly stretched out by reducing the size of the paving stones as they fall further away from the initial point of view. Sadly, however, a series of antique urns have been placed along one side of the walkway. Since they do not diminish in size there is a distortion between the real and the fake that is irritating. It seems a shame not to be bothered to have urns made that played in to the whole visual device.

Andrew Lawson originally planted his vista so as to enhance the effect further: he had yellow daffodils each side of the path, in hybrids of carefully selected declining size. But eventually he got bored with the number of daffodils, and replanted the borders with rather less contrivance, repeating in practice Anne Wareham's comment that 'I'm only prepared to play these games if they add to the pleasure of looking at the garden.'

It is remarkable how much difference to perspective well thought out formal trellises can make. The squarest garden can become almost any shape, as the rigour of line associated with trellis sets up expectations and prepares the eye to be fooled. Frolics, a company based in Winchester who live up to their name, supply perspective-warping trellises ready-made; and their catalogue should prove an inspiration. For further ideas, a study of Renaissance paintings is a good investment – the application of certain technical and totally artificial rules delivers, at least to the western-trained eye, an almost guaranteed effect, which could be laid out on garden earth in all sorts of materials, as well as on the walls that are all too often seen as a problem in the contemporary urban and suburban garden.

The problem of that wall is not a new one; as early as 1920 A.A. Milne was fretting about it, wittily:

At the back of my garden I have a high brick wall. To whom the wall actually belongs I cannot say, but anyway I own the surface rights on this side of it. One of my ideas is to treat it as the backcloth of a stage and paint a vista on it. A long avenue of immemorial elms, leading up to a gardener's lodge at the top of the wall – I mean at the end of the avenue – might create a pleasing impression....

But you have probably guessed already the difficulty in the way of my vista. The back wall extends into the gardens of the householders on each side of me. They might refuse to co-operate with me; they might insist on retaining the blank ugliness of their walls, or endeavour (as they endeavour now, I believe) to grow some unenterprising creeper up them; with the result that my vista would fail to create the necessary illusion when looked at from the side. This would mean that our guests would have to remain in one position, and even in that position they would have to stand to atten-tion – a state of things that might mar their enjoyment of our hospitality....

However there are other possibilities. Since there is no room in the garden for a watchdog and a garden, it might be a good idea to paint a phosphorescent and terrifying watchdog on the wall. Per-haps a watchlion would be even more terrifying – and, presumably, just as easy to paint. Any burglar would be deterred if he came across a lion suddenly in the back garden....

And if the worst comes to the worst – if it is found that no flowers (other than groundsel) will flourish in my garden owing to lack of soil or lack of sun – then flowers must be painted on the wall. This would have its advan-tages, for we should waste no time over the early and uninteresting stages of the plant, but depict it at once in its full glory. And we should keep our garden up to date. When delphiniums went out of season, we should rub them out and give you chrysanthemums; and if an untimely storm uprooted the chrysanthemums, in an hour or two we should have a won-derful show of dahlias to take their place....

One way or another, it should be possible to have something a little more interesting than mere bricks at the end of the estate.[15]

Milne's intention may have been humorous, but his problem was not; but as it happens many of his suggested solutions, along with others, have been tried, often to great effect. The painted, representational *trompe-l'oeil*, sometimes with added genuine 3-D effects, has a long history and appears to be making a come back.

In north Oxfordshire, Mrs Clark was confronted with a problem not dissimilar to Milne's: an extension to her house left her with a brick wall on which it seemed nothing would grow – not even the 'unenterprising creepers' disdained by Milne. The area was not large but was highly visible from other parts of the garden. A mural seemed a good solution, and the one she has ended up with – done by a neighbour without particular experience – is both well executed and well thought out.

Mrs Clark laid out a small 'formal' garden in font of the offending wall, with a (real) urn in the centre and clipped box hedges and an axial path running straight up to it. The foreground of the mural mirrors the garden and

Below
A bare Oxfordshire wall in Mrs Clark's garden now acts as a window into another world. References to Alice in Wonderland *are also found in other parts of the 'real' garden.*

Right

When executed with thought and skill, trompe-l'oeils *can be unbelievably realistic. The illusion of this urn is immeasurably improved by its setting, and by the matching of 'real' and 'fake'.*

continues it: a painted urn and tidy topiary run up to a high garden wall with a more open vista beyond. Mrs Clark did not stop with the naturalistic, however, for coming down the path and looking out of the picture is Alice, with her flamingo croquet mallet in her arms. The selection of Alice was not casual – the garden already contained both a croquet lawn and an outdoor chess game, and thus the references multiplied. 'Hidden' within the painting, like a child's puzzle, are other characters from the books; visual tricks within the visual trick. The sophistication of both idea and execution here should not deter anyone: this is not an expensive device nor one particularly difficult to execute – although considerable research was applied to the mundane business of sourcing the paints.

More complex *trompe-l'oeils* as a solution to Milne's 'end wall' problem are of course possible. The artist Roy Alderson has created an extreme example, which while it might not be to everyone's taste – including ours – does open spectacular ideas and opportunities. This *trompe-l'oeil* has three notable points. Firstly, the piece includes a 'real' horizontal balustrade and statue – actual stone objects that sit on a shelf and allow planting between them and the wall. Secondly, the painting has been executed with great technical skill to give dramatic results – pink stone effects have been painted on melamine, while steps, banisters and urns are acrylic on plaster. The third point addresses Milne's concerns about the neighbours' walls spoiling his illusions: heavy planting around, above and each side of the wall not only keep out whatever is 'next door', since presumably the wall either continues to the right and left of the *trompe-l'oeil* or hides something undesirable behind it, but also, perhaps more importantly, disguises the seams between the 'real' and the 'painted'.

Achieving the same effect, though on a smaller scale, Mrs Clark has grown a wisteria over and around her Alice picture, and this sort of framing – or perhaps anti-framing – technique seems almost universal to effective *trompe-l'oeils*. This may be the reason why they often give most pleasure when placed in an architectural context – within niches, such as the painted urns in the Palladian façades at Corpusty Mill or Andrew Lawson's 'seascape', or in niches and other spaces where the painting and the available flat surface can be coterminous. When Michelle Alles moved into her purpose-built suburban home in Wembley she found her brick end wall 'pretty drab'. By extending her *trompe-l'oeil* mural across the whole wall, rather than just painting the archway, she has effected a transformation that does not need additional framing or disguising, although she has in fact further softened the effect by planting.

In Cheltenham Mr and Mrs W. A. Bachelor took this idea to its logical conclusion by '*trompe-l'oeil*-ing' the whole of the garage that occupied the end of their small town garden. They built a colonnade, painted the windows and placed a mirrored arch to construct, part through visual illusion and part through 3-D effects, a whole classical portico. Once again, attention to detail paid off – painting the whole garage to match the rear wall of the house pulled the design together, which was essential in so small a garden.

Above

Bill Holloway has taken topiary a step further in his Gloucestershire front garden. The Irish yew is dressed in summer to the delight of passers-by, who now treat her as part of the community.

Such visual tricks are jokes not hoaxes. In none of these examples is the real intention to deceive, but more in the manner of a conjuring trick, to pretend to deceive, to create an illusion. But there does have to be that moment of confusion if the delighted amusement is to follow; if it is difficult to make a good joke of incongruity, as we have suggested, it is even harder to get this sort of visual trickery right. The risk so often pays off, however, and if the intellectual expense is high the actual financial outlay need not be. More of us should give it a go.

It can be very simple. Myra Tucker, in her extraordinary tiny garden just outside Bristol, has celebrated a family connection with the Arizona Desert. She fell in love with the giant cacti there, but could neither fit nor grow one in her garden, so her husband simply painted a 1.2-metre (4-foot) high one on the wall of their house for her. After it was completed, she discovered that it did not stand out as sculpturally as she had hoped and consequently looked a bit dull, so they outlined the painting with *barbed wire*. This is a wonderfully satisfactory joke – the spikes of the original plant giving focus to the artwork; and as an additional bonus it transpires that in the morning and late afternoon the sun shining at an oblique angle to the wall creates strange shadows. At virtually no cost the Tuckers have acquired a unique piece of garden 'sculpture' that has strong personal references for them, makes a humorous point about cacti and triggers memories of the fierce sun of the desert.

One place where these sorts of devices would be most effective is the shaded area outside many of our older basement flats. These areas create a real gardening problem: they can be viewed from two conflicting angles – close up at ground level from the semi-basement window, and from virtually overhead, with the inevitable foreshortenings and distortions. They usually lack sunlight and also, almost inevitably, lack soil. The chances of putting much in are reduced by highly practical concerns such as damp walls, plumbing and power access, so that even Milne's 'unenterprising creeper' presents problems. At the same time they are highly visible – every visitor and every passer-by will see and judge the house owner by the area. Meanwhile, the residents have a very dull view from their window. What areas do have, however, is a lot of wall; flat, smooth walls crying out, one might hope, for a bit of illusion, painted visual trickery. We have searched in vain for a truly creative interpretation of this common outdoor space, and would love to hear of any illuminating suggestions.

There is one particular form of horticulture which has never abandoned its own particular brand of wit: topiary. When Bacon wrote *Of Gardens* he already felt that the whole business had got out of control: he deplored the use of so many topiary hunts, animals and 'figures'. Endeavouring to restrain his readers from going too far in this direction, he urged them to confine themselves to geometrical lines and symmetrical shapes. Luckily he was only partially successful.

There are two sorts of topiary: the grand style, of which Bacon would have approved, and witty topiary, of which he was so scathing. The former requires a good deal of space and a long time to grow. It is fashionable at present to say that 'yew is not *that* slow growing', but frankly it is: 15 cm (6 inches) a year may not sound too slow, but for topiary you really need a dense thick fat hedge, not a single vertical twig. The best 'high' topiary gardens are made of yew and have had at least 50 years, and a *lot* of work, to mature. They are lovely and have a rich magic of their own, but they are not a solution for most of us. Unfortunately, this grand style has gained an ascendancy so that less high-minded species and forms are despised.

Below
Contrary to popular belief, topiary does not need to be serious or grand to be impressive. There is a trend for more whimsical subjects to be clipped and trained into increasingly bizarre shapes. A varied menagerie is kept in this garden on Rhode Island in the USA.

This is a shame because witty topiary, and the clipping of plants other than yew or box, is a source of real delight to its owners and of amusement and pleasure of a special kind to its beholders. It can work very effectively in gardens of all sorts and sizes and styles.

'High' topiary impresses by the mood of ancient solemn magic it creates – plus real admiration for the sheer hard work, the perfection of the concept, the execution and the minutely exact finish. 'Low' topiary does something quite different: although the hard work is still apparent and admired, representational topiary amuses precisely in the contrast between the plant, the 'natural', and the carving, the 'artistry', which is unnatural, artificial.

One of the things we are learning is just how many species can be topiarized or at least standardized and manipulated into mop-heads, umbrellas or lollipops. And how complex a design the more traditional topiary plants will carry. The bizarre multi-headed box 'trees' from Thomas Church's own 1930s garden hold out optimistic promise for the future, while santolina carved into grey sea waves invites wider experimentation and creativity.

In both Holland and the USA the skill of growing plants on wire frames, either as climbers or as annuals planted directly into the frames, which could be described as 'fake' topiary, is much more highly developed than in the UK. I suspect that the low esteem in which it is held here is a snobbish reaction to the seaside pier approach of the 1950s, where the most bizarre 'living statuary' became a sort of annual competition; but Susan Cunliffe-Lister's ivy 'wall', designed by Rupert Till on wire frames in the shape of chess pieces, leads one to hope that the technique could be made acceptable by a greater boldness. At the other end of the size range, the perfect sphere of sempervivums that hangs from the lamppost at the entrance to Barbara Watson's garden near Peterborough, looking entirely sculptural as though it were made of some previously undiscovered metallic substance, suggests that a little creative imagination could bridge the gap between grand yew and the hanging basket.

In passing we would like to know why, given the easy availability of light-weight containers, no one has combined the ancient and much admired topiary yew chess set with the equally charming giant chess game and created small-scale topiary chess pieces in pots that could be moved about – tiny dark green and golden box balls for pawns, for example.

The primary school at Clun in Shropshire, on the borders of England and Wales. has recently acquired a wonderful dragon, 9 metres (30 feet) long, designed and constructed locally, based on a metal frame with assorted climbers and plants set into woven willow lathes. It does seem unfair that grown-ups should be deprived of such living delights through a misplaced sense of dignity.

There is, however, one garden plant that is becoming more and more acceptable to play with, humorously or more ethereally, and that is lawn grass. The internationally mocked obsession that the British and American gardener is supposed to have about the perfect lawn makes this a specially fruitful arena for the more light-hearted. Some lawn effects are not so much witty as magical and will appear elsewhere in this book, but some are simply funny. Failing to mow your lawn for a couple of weeks so that a dawn carving of 'Happy Birthday' can greet your partner or child on awakening (especially if an upstairs bedroom window overlooks the lawn) seems to me a gift that no one could fail to be pleased with, even though the effect will be temporary. A miniature version of the Nazca lines, or an outline of the Eiffel Tower, might compensate for a failure to take your beloved to South America or Paris.

Lawns offer infinite potential for the expression of humour and personality and, as more and more lawnmowers have cutting levels that can be easily changed, the difficulties of construction and maintenance are reduced. Nor need grass swards be confined to the horizontal: often moving them, or restructuring them, does more than create a witty feature – it actually makes people think about the extraordinary

Opposite

Modern materials in brilliant colours have been used to create this lobster by Niki de Saint-Phalle, which was shown at the Galerie Beaubourg, Vence, France.

nature of grass, and especially of turf. In Johnny Woodford's already witty garden in Brighton there was no space for a traditional lawn so he moved it on to the sloping shed roof; The Avant Garden, a highly creative garden design and supply shop, is selling a lawn armchair; Ian Hodgson, editor of *The Garden* (the monthly journal of the Royal Horticultural Society), has created some wonderful turf flowerpots. He doubts that they would flourish on a very long-term basis, but as temporary features they have both charm and an element of witty surprise. Andrew Lawson has created the simplest of parterres by mowing, and not mowing, his lawn in geometric patterns. A new technique of spraying mud impregnated with grass seed on to pre-existing structures can create at least briefly magical effects, such as grassy flights of stairs and lavishly complex pictures on smooth stone or paved patios and courtyards.

Grass or lawn sculpture, sometimes associated with what is being called Land Art or Earthworks, is emerging as a serious art form, but it has its lighter moments. Lin Lervik created a huge recumbent *Mother Earth Sofia* for the 1997 Sofiero Garden Festival in Sweden – a woman sprawled on her back in the sun with her breasts, head, upper arms and knees emerging from the earth as though she were bathing. She was modelled in compressed peat and then overlaid with turf; a particularly nice touch was leaving her hair to grow long while the rest of her bulk was diligently clipped, and to plant tiny ivies for her ears,

Opposite
The Kasen Summers' garden in Connecticut, USA, was created by the innovative designer George Carter. This view through an ornate wooden gate is of the formal vegetable garden, which has an urn on a pedestal as its focus.

Left
Land art meets lawn care: a recumbent Mother Earth Sofia *was created by Lin Lervik for the 1997 Sofiero Garden Festival in Sweden. The sculpture was modelled in peat and then turfed, with detailed touches such as the longer hair and ivy ears adding further wit and subtle variation.*

providing a subtle variation. The remarkable refinement of her facial features under these circumstances is impressive and suggests a great deal of practice and skill, but simpler versions exist. James Pearce, on his farm in Maine, has solved the face problem by having his *Earthwoman* sprawled flat on her face with her arms splayed out and her buttocks open to the wind, suggesting fertility in its most basic form. Perhaps our favourite example of this style is the turf sleeping figure in a wrought iron bed at Rampisham in Dorset, which seems to capture so many of the elements that we have been discussing in this chapter. It is unexpected, incongruous, requiring ingenuity and skill and perfectly breaches the gulf between nature and nurture. Here the juxtaposition of perfectly 'mown' grass, the 'wild flower planting' of a 'neglected' orchard, and the entirely manufactured bed are given an extra little twist by our knowledge of how many old rusting metal beds just like this one contaminate the countryside, and an acknowledgement of the sleepy delight of sunny days in the garden.

George Carter is a garden designer who constructs elaborate ornate 'follies' and architectural effects that are often made out of quite temporary materials and highly painted. His work ranges widely, from a pale pink romantic windmill to the extraordinary garden he built in Connecticut for the Kasen Summerses, a family of art collectors. Here, highly dramatic white wooden trellised structures – boundary walls, lodge gates, pavilions and summerhouses – are laid on to a landscape of dense New England forest in a way that feels surreal and almost shocking. In his own garden, which is almost entirely free of flowering plants, he has constructed a complex series of sentry boxes, follies, summerhouses and pavilions, right down to a pink and white dog kennel that looks as though it was designed for an egotistical dachshund's dream of a fairy tale palace. Owing to a shortage of dogs, Carter is now planning to float it on his pond as a duck roost instead.

Carter is conscious of the problems that his style creates for other people who have difficulty in locating the influences and therefore don't seem to know how to see his pieces. (We tried him on 'Gothic?' and he answered, 'with a 'K' perhaps.') For him the influences are clear:

> The Landscape Movement of the mid-18th century is, to this day, the strongest influence in gardening, obliterating everything else before it and creating in modern minds the idea that it is a bad thing to shape nature for our own ends. I am trying to develop ideas as if the Landscape Movement had never occurred.

Perhaps, then, it is not surprising that, in his own garden, he is building a theatre – a rectilinear lawn surrounded by a high hedge with niches and dramatic lighting effects. When we asked him if he was going to employ actors and musicians, he said he really liked the idea of 'automata' - mechanical moving figures; a revival of the spirit of Pratolino in a modern, 'minimalist' style.

With this element of high performance in his work, it is not surprising that Carter's show gardens – he has exhibited at Chelsea since 1985, exploring the emblematic and symbolic aspects of garden design – are so satisfactory; always witty and thought provoking. On the whole, show gardens tend to be annoying, as they make impracticable suggestions for non-existent 'real' gardens. But in terms of garden spectacle, where instead of trying to 'instruct' the humble amateur they set out to stun or amuse their audience, they can occasionally work amazingly well.

Peter Styles of Lingard and Styles Landscapes produced a garden for Chelsea 1998 that, while it is almost impossible to imagine it existing in any reality whatsoever, was one such: a tiny kingdom of luxury and absurdity with a noble ceramic throne sculpted by Emma Lush on which one could believe oneself to be monarch of a royal kingdom. Here, a witty concept was carried through with extraordinary care – even the ceramic pots were shaped like crowns; the pool was dammed by a castellated slate wall through

Opposite

Emma Lush creates garden furniture that on first impression seems to be borrowed from inside the house. In actual fact, it is glazed ceramic. The juxtaposition is clever and the trick that has been played remains amusing.

which water tumbled; and the plants were systematically selected for their regal connections, by colour or name or association.

Of course not all jokes and tricks have to be *visual*. There are other sensory pleasures and other kinds of wit. On the whole we think of gardens as offering primarily visual pleasures, with – if plant catalogues are to be believed – a secondary theme of scent.

But perfume, like the visual aspects of flowers, has been used almost exclusively for romantic effect. Sue Prideaux is one of the few gardeners we have encountered who has found a wittier application for smell. In a 'hot' garden planted with colours and shapes associated with the East, she has edged her borders not with traditional lavender but with *Helichrysum italicum*, which when not in flower looks fairly similar but which produces a hot eastern scent, hence its common name – 'the curry plant'. The whole of this part of the garden takes on a smell so deeply associated with India that one notices the planting as well as being amused by the unexpected savour.

Gardens could also well be noisier. Bushell, following Bacon's example, had musicians follow him around his garden, to invoke mood and give delight. It is curious that although many people introduce artificial lighting into their gardens, very few seem to pay the same attention to music. Even without a full-scale automated orchestra, the wiring in of high quality stereo speakers would enhance garden evenings; particularly since volume can now be manipulated so easily with a remote control device.

On a roof garden in central London song birds apparently sing well into the night. The owner does not have an aviary – the birds were left free in the countryside, but their songs were taped and replayed on a loop system. First the bird song is barely noticeable, then it is pleasing, becomes curious or baffling, and finally the trick is exposed to the amusement and delight of the tricked.

Quite apart from music or bird song, tape recordings have another potential use. Many people want to have the music of running water in their gardens, but running water is one of the most difficult features to create satisfactorily in a small-sized garden: there are more bad 'water features' loose in domestic gardens, striving to look 'natural' and failing dismally, than is pleasant to think about. Fountains and formal pools can and do work, but the babbling brook effect, unless you are lucky enough to have an authentic stream to start with, is nearly (not quite) impossible. What is the case against tape recording a real one and playing it back through well-concealed speakers? The sissirations of bamboos could also make a passably similar noise to running water – or at least a pleasing alternative. But if the Porter's Lodge can handle a water organ, then surely modern technology can deliver some more of the effects that the High Renaissance managed with only servants and hydraulics?

The style we are trying to sum up in this chapter has perhaps been best articulated by the great contemporary garden designer David Stevens. In a letter to the British magazine *The Garden Design Journal* in spring 1999, he wrote:

> Boy, were we pompous last time in the autumn 1998 issue … keep at it; there is humour out there somewhere (not necessarily lavatorial) and it belongs in the garden – lighten up!

Reflecting on Reflections

And moving thro' a mirror clear,
That hangs before her all the year,
Shadows of the world appear.

ALFRED, LORD TENNYSON, 'The Lady of Shalott' (1842)

R EFLECTION IS ONE OF THOSE PLEASING WORDS that have a double meaning. To 'reflect' is to mirror, to repeat an image, light playing a double role, upside down, back to front, but yet serene – a calm visual playfulness that delights by emphasizing its own peace and serenity. Reflections can be both witty and amusing – they throw up illusions and questions on perspective that challenge how we see the world, while appealing to the serious, intellectual aspects of wit. It is perhaps no coincidence that mental reflection is often stimulated by a still pool of water or a well-placed mirror. But to 'reflect' is also to think calmly about something or nothing; to sit or lie half dozing while the mind turns something over calmly and serenely. Religious retreats advertise themselves by offering the world weary 'a time for reflection'. And for many people this is the primary purpose of their garden – an escape, an oasis of peace and privacy. For those who see their gardens in this spirit it may well be more appropriate to draw on still water than on bubbling, gurgling, laughing water. In reflecting images, mirroring the world above it, still water also reflects the meditations of the gardener.

Water is perhaps the feature most people would like to have in their gardens. Unfortunately, there are more unsatisfactory water features in gardens up and down the land than there are ill thought through schemes of other kinds. The sad fact is that unless you are blessed with natural water, it is extremely hard to get a good natural effect, especially on a small scale.

Part of the problem is that people want water for several different reasons which, on the whole, are in conflict with each other. 'Natural' ponds to encourage wildlife and make a congenial home for aquatics and bog plants can be very difficult to maintain. Where they occur naturally the plants accommodate to inevitable changes in water level, but nothing looks worse than the all too frequent rim of black plastic liner, which emerges whenever there is a dry spell. It is hard to get a natural-looking shape, and harder still to create artificially the surrounding area of damp bog. When these ponds are not swamped by some successful 'natural' weed, they tend to get dirty, murky and even smelly. Damming, digging or diverting where there is a water supply is a very different matter. Capability Brown was so named because when

Opposite
In the Mythic Garden at
Stone Farm, Freedom
by Benjamin Venn is
exquisitely positioned
over this dark pool. The
double image provokes
appropriate reflection on
the artist's theme.

70

he came to site at the preplanning phase he would assess its 'capabilities'. If there was water, he would find a way to engineer lakes, canals and waterfalls, but he had the distinct advantage of *never* wanting a 'natural' look, preferring a stylized classical one.

There are various ways of using water in the garden, which are often manageable and desirable in themselves, but well nigh impossible to combine. Moving water, fountains and falls fill a garden with the sound of laughter; still water reflects, it offers soothing double visions and serenity – but very few schemes can do both at once. If you don't have the space for more than one water feature, it is important to decide which you prefer.

On the whole moving water, for its sound and refreshing effects, has found more favour in the contemporary garden than still water, but the magical qualities of reflection should not be discounted.

The earliest gardeners, from the lands between the two rivers, ancient Mesopotamia – now Iran and Iraq – modelled their landscapes on Paradise itself. Their idea of paradise was secluded, shady, geometrical and containing water – usually canals running out from or in to a central pool – which was designed for reflection in both senses of the word. The Islamic empire took over these ideals and brought them through North Africa into Europe. The Moorish gardens of southern Spain endure as horticultural masterpieces, although curiously their underlying concepts have not been as much used as points of reference in modern

Below

The Christie Sculpture Garden created by George Carter for Chelsea 1999 is a formal design that makes the best use of water and lighting to produce an environment conducive to reflection.

gardens as one might have expected. While the influences of oriental gardens, Japanese and Chinese, have been extensive (if sometimes regrettable), little of the pure serenity of Islamic garden style has been adopted. In recent years, however, there have been a few show gardens at Chelsea that have picked up on this theme: The Yves Saint-Laurent garden in 1996 was almost slavish in its North African references, itself a reflection of Saint-Laurent's famous garden near Marrakech; the colours of bright sunshine and the desert planting of cacti and other succulents around a still pool was meant to make one think directly of Morocco. In 1999 George Carter showed a garden sponsored by Christie's, the fine art auctioneers, which developed the Moorish concept in a more northern, cool manner, with a long dark canal reflecting a pale planting of greys and whites. Serene and still, it stood out as a direction well worth exploring. The potency of Carter's credo of designing 'as though the Landscape Movement had never taken place' showed its strength here – he was using a number of classical points of reference to create a completely contemporary garden, but the Moorish element was a strong one. A third Chelsea show garden worth mentioning in this context, as well as in the previous chapter, was Peter Styles' award-winning garden in 1998, sponsored by Blakedown Landscapes. Although the references were less direct, the idea of a throne overlooking a smooth and reflective pool was also drawn from this tradition.

Out in the real world, this idea of geometrical gardens centred on reflecting water has been less utilized. This neglect is a shame because it can prove extremely effective: in Herefordshire the Hattats' carefully designed garden at Arrow Cottage contains a 'rill'. A very narrow, perhaps 25 centimetres (10 inches) wide, canal runs for 27 metres (30 yards) or so absolutely straight down from a paved courtyard in front of a two-storey folly or summerhouse, painted a strong Tuscan yellow. The rill descends a series of wide steps, but the water flows slowly so the flat stretches are calm and still. On either side of the canal the ground is paved with only occasional planted containers and the whole area is shut in with high yew hedges, creating a long simple corridor. Walking up the corridor one becomes engaged in an extraordinary game of reflection. Each time you climb one of the small steps the angle of reflection is changed – so that although the actual summerhouse comes nearer, the reflected summerhouse in the rill appears to retreat before you. Arriving in the paved courtyard you no longer see the reflection and as you turn and look behind you you can still see the canal but no reflection; instead the far end of the alley is framed by a tall single plume of fountain set into a paved circle. The yew hedge and the careful placing of this feature makes it a surprise from whichever end you see it first, but a very different quality of surprise: here the almost magical power of reflection and the ideas of the Moorish garden come together to spectacular effect.

There are of course other ways of using still water and its reflective power. John Tordoff has a typical, long narrow urban garden in East London. It is an amazing garden for a number of reasons. It is divided rigorously in half. At the house end is an Italianate paved terrace contained within a heavily planted 'wall' with a formal pool and fountain, and tightly clipped geometrical topiary. At the far end of this section is a rose arch which invites the viewer to explore further without revealing much of what they may expect to find. The rigorous formality is undercut, however, by what Tordoff calls 'clutter': a range of containers and other architectural features, mainly garnered from rubbish tips, and two white china doves decorate the fountain in the centre of the pond, which sprays into a bowl raised above the surface of the pool so that it does not disturb the reflective stillness.

The other half of the garden could not be a greater contrast: it is a Japanese landscape; a garden that aims at a Japanese ambience rather than a philosophically correct pastiche. From a tea house at the far end a tiny, crystal-clear river winds through the centre of a jewel green field. The bizarre bright green is created by an unbroken planting of *Soleirolia soleirolii* ('Mind your own Business'), decorated only with miniature

rocks, while around this circular landscape is a lavish arrangement of Japanese plants. The whole is scaled almost perfectly to the river, which is perhaps 25 cm (10 inches) at its widest.

But the truly magical nature of this garden is the linking of the two halves. In different forms – the fountain and the river – both these gardens are dominated by their moving water, but in the centre there is still, reflecting water. John Tordoff has taken the main pathway up the side of the garden, so there is no obvious vista to connect the two gardens; instead between them there is an open sheet of water – a pond that runs the whole width of the garden, and then breaks through the walled boundary (the other half of the pond is in fact in the neighbours' garden). The water can be crossed, but the bridge – at the end of the side path – is not visible from either main garden. It is impossible to tell how large this pond might be; it picks up the green reflections from both the Japanese and the Italian scenery and carries them away into

a never–never land. It is equally impossible to guess how deep the pond is; although some of the surface is covered with *Aponogeton distachyus* (South African water hawthorn) and with *Sagittaria sagittifolia* (arrowhead). Below the surface, roach occasionally swim past, suggesting depth, but the reflections distort and refract the smoothness. The whole garden is so tightly organized and managed that this sheet of water breaking out, getting away from the restrictions imposed by boundary walls and the length and narrowness of the whole, has a totally magical effect, which somehow puts the eccentricities of the two main sections of the garden into perspective. It is sad that this solution – coming to terms with one's neighbours – is not more common than it seems to be; since it delivers exactly the contrast between enclosure and openness that is so satisfying.

Working on an entirely different scale, the novelist Sue Prideaux, whose helichrysum hedge was mentioned in the previous chapter, has used reflection to an equally magical effect at Selehurst in Sussex. Sue Prideaux's garden is in many ways a contemporary rendition of the 18th-century landscape garden. Indeed, at the furthest and lowest point the garden terminates in a theatre, a deep circular declivity designed as a tribute to Alexander Pope. Around the house are a series of garden rooms, but away from the house the garden converts itself into 'park', running down a valley that she has successfully dammed and flooded to create five substantial pools, so that one looks down on the water from higher points, or from the very bottom upwards into the garden planted with rhododendrons and azaleas, plus euchryphia and other fine trees. Selehurst Garden took the brunt of the 1987 hurricane, however, and Sue Prideaux lost over 100 mature trees, particularly those on the higher ribs. To console herself she built a folly; a truly 18th-century fake Gothic building with shell-lined walls inside, which sits on the very top and edge of a steep slope down to the pools. Behind it she dug out a formal round pond, whose outlet flows across the folly floor and down a stepped cascade, lined in black and white pebbles, into the pond beneath. The positioning of the folly is key to its success because it is fully and perfectly reflected in the pool below it from various points lower down the garden. It is also reflected in the pond behind it, but from a totally different angle. At Selehurst the reference point is Stourhead, a style of gardening that we address very little in this book, but the wit of the folly and the detailed delicacy of its construction and positioning move it from mere 'copy cat' reproduction to a stylish statement of its own; seen through the complicated planting, including a yew circle, from the house approach it looks delightful, seen from below reflected in the pools, it is entrancing.

Another enviably magical combination of improbable building and reflecting water can be seen in the swimming pool designed by and for himself by Scott Johnson in Bridgehampton, New York. Johnson claims to have built it to combine two of his pet obsessions – the folly and the beach entry swimming pool. But it is impossible not to see a Venetian fantasy at work here, together with the childhood dream of jumping out of a window or off a balcony into safe but exciting water – the pool is 3.4 metres (11 feet) deep under the balcony to enable him to do just that.

The element of fantasy is greatly increased by the fact that the pool comes as a surprise – you approach the folly, or cottage, from the opposite side to the pool, up a curved paved series of steps, across a flagstone patio and through French doors. From this angle it appears to be a single-storey structure, consisting of an elegant sitting room – a slightly larger than average summerhouse. The pool remains invisible until you step out on to the balcony, although the quality of light inside is enhanced by the bright clarity of the water and sunshine reflecting off it. From the pool side of the building the basement windows, only inches above the water level, increase the sense of drowning. Perhaps the overall effect could have been heightened even more by simplifying the materials used; there are an awful lot of them: quartz stone for the cottage, flagstones for the patio and the pool's coping, and river rocks and Japanese-style garden stones for the beach and granite boulders that make ornamental edges. But Johnson defends this choice, saying that the materials are visually linked through colour (blue-greys and earthy shades) and shape. It is worth noticing also that, although the picture shows a spectacular and summery reflection, the mirror effect would have been increased if the bottom of the pool had been darker. On this, though, Johnson has no apologies: 'Some people like a pond bottom to be dark and disappear, but here I wanted clarity, the pure harmony of water and stone.... It's meant to be fun.'

Swimming pools are quite common in the USA (where there are over 300,000 private ones, 113,500 of them in southern California) and many of them are designed not just to swim in but to be a part of the garden – Bacon's bathing pools. The way they reflect light and shade can be a part of their effect, particularly if the pool is situated among trees and has plants – chosen carefully as not many species enjoy a regular drenching with chlorinated water – close to the edges.

Even the more romantic notion of the moat, which creates wonderful reflections binding house and garden into each other in a third magical realm, has not really found a modern expression. Perhaps we have let ourselves get over worried by the sinister sound of 'rising damp', although modern liners and similar developments should solve the problem in most cases. At Sutton Place, Jellicoe brought the water right up to one side of the old Tudor mansion house, which – at least in that direction – one had to leave over stepping stones; to walk across the surface of water that is reflecting a lovely house or tree has a quality of magical tranquillity worth developing.

You do not need acres of land or millions of pounds to create water features that provide interesting or even magical reflections. The tiniest pools of water, properly sited and arranged, will act as mirrors, pulling pieces of sky down to earth or doubling magically the pleasure that a flowering plant or delicate branch can offer. The classical Japanese *tsukubai,* water basins, could have moving or still water, but the still ones were often placed so that they would not reflect pleasingly unless the guests humbled themselves to bend down to wash. This idea repeats the ancient classical Greek myth of Narcissus, who leaned over a pool and was so enchanted by his reflection that he refused to leave and was turned into a flower.

It is worth remembering then that reflective water in a garden is not hard to come by, but to maximize its effectiveness there are some points worth receiving serious consideration. If reflection is what you want then you need to organize your water so that it is not excessively exposed to wind and can be filled and emptied as gently as possible, to keep the surface smooth. The darker and stiller the water the more it will act as a mirror; the greater the contrast between the light above and the darkness beneath the surface of the water the stronger and more precise the reflection will be – so reflecting water needs to be placed somewhere that is not too dark or shaded. Despite Johnson's fabulous blue swimming pool, you are most likely to get good reflections with a black or other dark shade of lining. The standard black polythene pool lining is highly suitable for this purpose, especially if it is laid as smoothly as possible. Where the intention is to keep the water very clean, as in a swimming pool, the colour of the sides and bottom will make an enormous difference to the effect, but for a garden feature this may not be important.

Anyone who has seen the extraordinarily pure reflections of mountains and trees that a still evening in the highlands of Scotland will draw out of a sea loch knows that if the water is deep enough it will effectively absorb all the light and, whatever the bottom is like, and however clean or murky the water is, it will appear to be dark and flat. But most of us do not have that kind of depth. Nancy McAvoy's swimming pool, which we described in the chapter on laughter, requires clean water as it is designed for swimming in. It could only be 1.2 metres (4 feet) deep for mundanely practical reasons, but the dark lining and the black tiles under the coping make it look deeper and increase its reflectivity.

Discoloration of the water itself does not inhibit reflection. The water does not have to be deep – a skin will do if the surface it covers is smooth and dark enough. In the illustration here the slab, barely covered by the water, is dark red marble and the effect is stunning: polished marble has, at the very least, a semi-reflective quality of its own, which keeping it wet obviously enhances. There is just enough water to pick up the sky and tree-branches, and give an unexpected magical effect, which works particularly well because we tend to think of marble as a very formal, if not grandiose, material so that its woodland setting has the additional frisson of the unexpected.

Above all, reflection works by very simple visual rules, as we all know from looking in mirrors: what you see in a reflecting surface depends with great precision on what angle you look into it from. Since still water is always and necessarily horizontal, it is possible to place your water, or the object that you wish to reflect, with great accuracy once you have decided on the point of view – or views – from which you most want to observe it. The sculptor Ben Nicholson designed a huge white wall, geometric and commanding, for the pool garden at Sutton Place. This garden had originally been designed and planted by Gertrude Jekyll, but the sculpture was added much later and with a great deal of thought. The formally shaped pool lies low in the garden: the visitor enters at a higher level – on a raised grass dais that runs around the whole garden. The sculpture has been placed precisely at the same height as the visitor and at the exact distance from the pool to allow its reflection to appear in full on the very edge of the pool at that moment of entry. If the entrance was anywhere else in the garden the effect would not be achieved. The reflection is heightened by the end of the pool itself being carved to 'mirror' the design of the sculpture. It is this care and sensitivity that turns natural reflection into a conjuring trick, and it is worth spending considerable time working out exactly what you want reflected and from where. For instance, a tree right beside a pool will reflect the overreaching branches when you are at the pool side. If you want the tree reflected from a more distant point of view, it must be planted further from the bank.

Obviously, plants *on* the surface will break up the reflections, although this need not be a bad thing – there is something strangely wonderful in having a perfect reflection broken up by an actual 'floating' object: it creates a third dimension, provoking thought and delight. This triple effect can work especially well if whatever lies on the reflecting surface is itself too flat to make further reflections – such as lily pads or fallen leaves. Stepping stones across a reflecting surface invite the observer into a mysterious world, poised between the dark depths and the bright heights.

However, water can reflect in other ways than holding up a mirror to the world above it. In Malibu, Jennifer and Kenneth Chiate's swimming pool reflects very differently: it mirrors the ocean beyond it, pulling in the sea and sky and making them part of the pool. This particular effect is called an 'infinity edge', its name alone worth reflecting upon. In point of fact, the water does not pour away endlessly over the rim and into the ocean, but falls only a few feet into a collecting basin set in the cliff side, whence it is pumped back through filters and re-enters the pool. The designer, Pamela Burton, kept the whole area around the pool low and clean so that more normal reflections did not interfere with the huge view and the blue surface of the pool which mirrors it.

As well as holding reflecting images, water also reflects light itself. Large stretches of water brighten the quality of light around them; which, to move from the sublime to the ridiculous, is why people have to be so careful about sunburn if they are spending a clear bright day on a boat; they are getting a double dose of sunlight. Even quite small pools can illuminate shady corners if they can catch even a little of the sun or the bright sky. When sharp light is reflected off water it can cast the precise opposite of shadow, making what, as children, we called the 'Tinkerbell effect', dancing sparks of light. This reflection can, like so many other optic effects, be managed by the thoughtful gardener. For the sharpest display of dancing points of light you do need movement in the water; ideally you want to create quite sharp-edged small waves, offering angled surfaces to the light source. The sun can do this on, for example, a lake; but in a garden it is important to manage and control the effect. In John Last's grotto, where the angles of light and the surfaces it encounters have been so carefully thought through, the initial sensation of total darkness is alleviated by the very curious movement of the reflections of light on the water – the whole enclosed space feels as though it was alive, moving, jiggling, in the way the light is played off the tiny fountain and thrown against the dark and irregular walls.

The reason why oyster shells were used so extensively in grottoes, cascades and fountains in the 17th and 18th centuries was because their mother-of-pearl inner surfaces are light reflective to a high degree, but at the same time their concave shape and irregularity means that the movement of light off them through running water is always random. The 'folly' at the Porter's Lodge has a substantial waterfall pouring over large oyster shells; the dark blue edges of the shells break up the light so that their translucent inner surfaces can reflect it. The fall is arranged to catch the sun while the watchers, seated on a bench with their back to the light source, are continually refreshed by the ever changing light show. In another part of the garden, water flows over lead – not a smooth sheet, but one that has been hammered into diamond-shaped patterns that again break up the fall of water. The reflective qualities of the lead are different from those of the shells, less sparkling perhaps but more intense and strange.

Variations of this effect – with falling water against a dark smooth surface, such as a wall, and a strong light source – would seem an almost perfect feature for a garden at night, now that control over the direction and power of lighting is so easily achievable.

Thinking about gardens and reflection we do tend to think 'water', but there are a great many other materials that have some of the same qualities of both reflection and refraction, which are much easier to maintain, and can be used at different angles from the horizontal one that still water requires. They all have effects of their own, and should not be seen simply as 'faked' water. Although one of the neatest and simplest examples we have come across is indeed entirely fake. Water creates special problems in roof gardens, as joists often cannot sustain the weight. When Anthony Henn was creating a roof garden for a Malaysian client, he simply *painted* a small pond on to the ground and then planted it up as though it were real. Normally, however, this sort of literal replication is not the best approach. As we become increasingly aware of how precious water is, and how it should not be wasted, we need to become more creative in achieving the much desired 'water feel' in our gardens.

In an experimental water-economical garden at Capel Manor in Essex, the designer – whose brief was explicitly to be water sensitive – used a stainless steel plate to replace the more traditional small pond. This proved an excellent alternative, surprisingly convincing and giving all the light, reflection and serene calm of 'the real thing'. Here, the stainless steel was being used in deliberate imitation of water rather than as a design material in its own right, but it generated curiosity and ideas. Used vertically, for example, behind a fairly open planting, it could produce the whole mood of water but – because of the angle – with an entirely new feel of its own. Stainless steel is heavy of course, and would presumably need regular cleaning, but so do ponds. Given the chronic maintenance problems of the average garden water feature, and bearing in mind that Bacon thought that standing pools should be cleaned by hand *daily*, stainless steel would seem to score rather highly, even as a simple substitute for still water.

Its reflective qualities could also be used in ways that water cannot: stainless steel makes wonderful plant containers, as the chimney lining tubes at Scypen in Devon show, generating a brightness – both of light and of mood. Their clean lines and absolute replicability suggest considerable possibilities for bringing a contemporary formalism and structure to the ubiquitous planting pot. In wind vanes and pennants the

Right

A faulty chimney liner was the starting point for this highly distinctive composition of metal and plants. The reflective images are so clear that it almost seems as if the foliage forms an integral part of the container.

shiny modern feel of stainless steel offers an interesting alternative to wrought iron – catching and tossing light as it moves in the breeze. Roger Last at Corpusty Mill has also been considering the possibilities of using aluminium for similar ends, but has been finding it hard to get much useful information about how aluminium will respond to having water poured over it. This is one of the on-going problems of using non-traditional or experimental materials in the garden. Will aluminium (or some other substance) last well? oxidize? turn green? kill plants? dull away completely?

Slate is another, more organic, material that has interesting reflective qualities; wet, smooth slate can indeed look very like grey, brooding water. Slate has been used, like stainless steel, to imitate water directly – dry streams and paths of loose-laid slate chips have provided the atmosphere of a stream without the inherent problems. Smoother, more formal slate patios and terraces can create a powerful atmosphere and throw off a dark reflection both ominous and beautiful.

The Chiates' infinity edge pool described earlier has a smooth paved surround. To keep the mood of intense light and the reflections of ocean and swimming pool, the paving was first painted to match the pool lining (itself chosen to match the ocean) and then given a black silicone carbonate finish so that it sparkles like water.

One material that is moving into the garden with very satisfactory results is glazed ceramics – exotic tiling, in vivid light-refracting colours and in mosaic designs. Once again, these are used, as Bacon wanted them to be, as pool liners, but also as 'pool alternatives'.

It still seems a little strange that glazed ceramics have found their way into gardens more easily than a far cheaper, more readily available and equally design-worthy material: glass. Glass seems to have almost everything going for it: it comes in any colour you want, any size you want, almost *any* shape you want – flat, curved, as small as glass beads and as huge as Crystal Palace. It is reasonably economical and wonderfully flexible. We use bottle glass daily but do not recycle it very imaginatively. Simply up-ended on stakes, coloured bottles can make an extraordinary boundary fence. Driven into the ground they make wonderful border edges. At Scypen in Devon, John and Ann Bracey have explored the use of old bottles in various structures in their garden. John Bracey says that he started using old wine bottles to create a luminous and reactive surface, but soon discovered that there was a whole technology and mathematics involved. To create regular courses it was important to use bottles of the same size, as he has done to make a drinks alcove and table (a rather charming joke). He is now constructing a children's den out of bottles, which will when finished be the shape of a bottle – perhaps with a clear glass stopper to let in more light. The lower courses are made of 1.5 litre (2½ pint) wine bottles and the higher ones of standard-size wine bottles. He has discovered as he works that the shape of the bottle design he has chosen will always result in the total number of bottles required being a prime number. When finished the interior will be plastered so that the open necks of the bottles create the only source of light; over 1,000 sparkling green eyes will watch his grandchildren in their illuminated playhouse.

Beyond bottles, glass offers an extraordinary range of potential effects. Prisms refract light and break it into colours – as the ones hanging on the Tree of Peace in Ivan Hicks' Garden in Mind demonstrate. It can be stone-washed so as to offer no danger and used like gravel for paths, but as the glass surfaces catch and refract the light while also being semi-transparent, it creates a totally different and more childlike atmosphere. In Herne Hill, South London, Jonathan and Jo Baillie have brought light and colour into their garden without any loss of privacy by inserting stained glass panels into their boundary fence. In Kettering, Northamptonshire, the novelist and publisher J.L. Carr brought a much-loved tree back to life by hanging glass leaves from its dead branches. At the Chauffeur's Flat in Surrey, the Richens have created delicate and intricate spiders' webs with tiny glass beads like dew drops, as well as other shining substances

REFLECTING ON REFLECTIONS

Left
This mirrored archway,
decorated with mosaic
tiles and slightly covered
with plants, gives the
impression that the
garden continues beyond
the wall. It is particularly
effective if approached
from an angle.

to represent the spider and its prey. Round glass balls in various sizes can be used as a 'mulch' for plant containers, as gazing balls, as statuary, and as *objets trouvés* lying in the grass. Modern glass bricks make spectacular external walls – and, returning to the watery theme with which we started, water flowing over clear glass or even slightly coloured glass bricks generates an unrivalled feeling of coolness and light as well as an apparent unsupported wall of water perpetually flowing downwards like something from an Escher drawing. In all these cases the glass reflects, either images or light, pulling new dimensions of space, brightness, sparkle and purity into the garden.

And of course, glass makes mirrors, which takes us back to where we started. Mirrors reflect. More reliably – and nowadays more flexibly – even than still water, mirrors bounce back light and space and images. Mirrors can illuminate dark corners, expand narrow spaces, trick the eye and amuse their beholder.

Mirrors can deliver *trompe-l'oeil* effects from the extremely simple to the magically complex or highly sophisticated: they will do so reliably, reasonably cheaply and permanently. They are not difficult to construct, need only cleaning as far as maintenance goes, and unfailingly add a special element of surprise and delight to any garden.

The most straightforward thing a mirror can do is persuade the mind that it is seeing double (or more) the amount of space that is really there. At the most basic level, if you were coming down the steps into an urban sub-basement area and the wall facing you was mirrored, it would reflect the wall parallel to the steps themselves, thus suggesting an area twice the size. If both end walls were mirrored or partly mirrored, the effect would be replicated, since mirrors reflect reflection as efficiently as they reflect their primary objects – which is why grand ladies had three-faced mirrors with movable wings on their dressing tables, and why the hairdresser holds a hand mirror behind you so that you can see the back of your head in the mirror in front of you.

By a slightly more complicated arrangement a mirror can suggest a whole distance, or a further garden beyond the real boundaries. The simplest version of this is the mirrored arch. Peter has designed a country garden for Richard Coles, the BBC presenter. He wanted a fairly straightforward plan of flowerbeds and grass, laid out on a basic rectangle; but the garden contained an awkward narrow corner running between the garage and the house. Quite apart from the fact that it was small, cramped and going nowhere, it also contained the oil tank, the pedestrian door to the garage, and the only window to one of the ground-floor rooms – so access and light had to be available. It ended abruptly in a high wall, which could not be demolished as it gave on to a remarkably uncharming farmyard. Peter designed a Mediterranean garden with terracotta pots and gravel paths leading both to the necessary door and straight up to the wall, on to which a mirror in the shape of a doorway was fixed; a vine was planted to grow over the edge of the mirror to hide the mountings. Now when you drive up to the house you have the sensation that the garden opens out beyond the doorway, which reflects the path, the terracotta pots and the trees. Of course this impression does not withstand detailed examination, but it does not need to: first you are fooled and then you are amused at having been fooled, and the whole effect is delightful.

This arch is not of course unique – John Tordoff has a mirrored arch in the narrow pathway that leads up the side of his garden; it makes the path feel wider. Roger Last has an arch inside his grotto, which is rather more disturbing in its effect as the observer has already been disorientated by the darkness and the scattered diffusion of the light inside. Mr and Mrs Bachelor's 'classical' garage, already described in the previous chapter, has a mirrored arch behind a statue as its focal point; the arch picks up the water extending back into the building and makes the statue appear to be in the centre of a more spacious pond.

There are more sophisticated interpretations of this trick. Jill Billington in her book *Town Gardens* describes a design she made for clients in London. The plot she had to work with was dark and cramped, so she created two mirrored arches. One faced the entrance to the garden, which was down a short flight of steps, and was positioned slightly to one side so that visitors would not immediately see themselves but instead a small pool with a carp fountain, apparently in a garden beyond the boundary wall. In fact this fountain was tucked in beside and below the steps. This mirror served another purpose too – the kitchen window of the house looked out into the garden, and the mirror allowed the hosts, busy in the kitchen, to see the whole of their garden and the dispositions of their guests as they arrived. The second mirror provided an axis running from a side gate right across the garden and apparently doubling its width. In both cases Billington ran the paths right up to the wall, and added short pergolas, which again drew the eye down the path and directly into the mirror. She emphasizes, as we would, that these effects work best when the edge of the mirror is disguised in some way.

The Macolls' garden in North London takes this sort of trickery a stage further. Their garden is located near the Regent's Canal – a 19th-century waterway that nearly encircles North London. The canal's towpath now provides one of the most pleasant urban walks in the city. Being an urban canal it is crossed frequently by bridges, many of which are low and arched. Thus this view of smooth stretches of reflecting water contained within architectural straight banks and intersected by low arches is not only well known to many Londoners, but also associated with one of the more agreeable contemplative urban pleasures. The Macolls' pulled the canal and all its associations into their garden. First a canal was constructed, dissecting the garden slightly more than halfway down, and running completely straight, with a paved area, like a towpath, each side of it. A small arched bridge was built to allow access to the far end of the garden, where a summerhouse was placed. Where the 'canal' – at each end – ran into the wall, bricked arches were constructed and the inner curve mirrored. Thus it seems that the canal flows right through the garden, under the anticipated arched bridges; the mirrors carry it under the boundary walls and, since there is a mirror at each end, wherever you view it from it appears that the canal runs away into the distance, just as the real one does. The surface of the canal water is lower than the 'towpath' and the rest of the garden, the arches have been kept very low and the mirrors have been set at right angles to the water, so it is unlikely that visitors will actually see their own reflection in the mirrors, although they may well see them in the water itself. Meanwhile, from the house and from the summerhouse they have a long view of peaceful water and a sense of light, space and distance.

Another way in which mirrors can be used to increase a sense of size is to place them on both sides of a corner: a single triangular bed can be made to look like a perfectly symmetrical square using mirrors. (Judy Wiseman has created a lavender parterre by this method.) But here a word of warning should be issued – for such effects to work best the longer observers can be deluded the happier they will be when they discover their folly; if the first thing they see as they approach the mirror is *themselves*, albeit in reverse, their sense of illusion will be shattered too soon. If the mirror is not high enough, so that they see only their own legs, they will not be able to enter into the magic. Make your mirrors tall enough and try to place them so that the guests do not walk straight up to them. With right-angled mirrors it is also quite difficult to disguise the join, so an unattractive vertical black line appears to run up the centre of the garden. This problem could be avoided by, for example, placing a small tree or artwork in the corner.

None the less, all rules are made to be broken. In the town garden created by Charles Jencks and his late wife Maggie Keswick (see opposite) the two side walls have mirrored gates in them, which are divided into panes like old-fashioned sash windows. The panes below the line of the dividing wall are mirrored, but those above, like the trellis each side of them, are left open so that the landscape behind the garden wall is revealed. This would appear to breach the suggestion of the previous paragraph, but in fact the result is satisfaction and interest. This is partly because the mirrors are not seen from a distance or straight on. It is

Opposite

The saying 'The future is behind you' is given actual meaning by the mirrored panes that glaze this 'Mystery Gate' in a London garden created by Charles Jencks and Maggie Keswick.

Below

The tiny mirror in the bottom of this nest of sticks is just enough to surprise the person who peers into it. It provides a slightly startling, but amusing, use of reflection.

also because the whole of this garden design is so complicated, tricky, intellectually demanding in the best sense of that word, and disorientating that the viewer's trust in his or her own capacity to see straight is undermined. The focal point of the garden, especially when viewed as it is designed to be from a first-floor window that opens so widely as to become a balcony, is of a pergola or arbour made of a modernistic arch, in which the mirrored planes are angled to distort material reality as well as to catch the light. Once the mind and senses are sufficiently boggled, there is little need to worry about naturalism or delusion.

Mirrors, of course, do not need to stay still. A hinged mirror screen allows you to change the view, catch the light or repeatedly transform the whole atmosphere by simply realigning the mirrors. At the same time as extending the garden in front of it, the screen closes out whatever is behind, and in itself provides an interesting focal point, elegant and modern.

Even very small pieces of mirror can play delightful tricks. In the garden of Kerscott House, near Barnstable in Devon, Jessica Duncan used some old branches and twigs from a fallen tree to form a small piece of land art. By building up and weaving the sticks together she created a 'natural' wooden mound, about 60 cm (2 feet) high, something between a nest and a pot. This structure has a round hole in the top that invites the curious to look in, and at the bottom is a mirror. When you peer in, you see two eyes looking out at you – a slightly startling but amusing use of reflection.

And finally a mirrored effect so fantastic that perhaps it belongs with magical rather the reflective gardens. Raf Fulcher and Elizabeth Tate's County Durham Garden, Wrekenton, is 24 metres (80 feet) long. A third of the way down the garden they constructed a dividing wall, which is dominated on one axis by a long narrow path that leads straight from the main door of the house to the wall. Beyond it is an apparent continuation of the path at a raised level. High planting is brought close to the side of the path, making the nearer end of the gravelled alley look dark and closely framed. Beyond the first wall the path can be seen continuing, now marked by conical clipped box hedges, which keep the eye moving steadily to a gazebo, at the final boundary wall. A complex stone arch, almost like a gazebo, surmounts the wall and looks down over the whole garden. The arch is not open, as it appears to be, but mirrored, although it is sufficiently high not to reflect any of the garden back to someone looking up. For a few moments on a few days, when the sun is at precisely the right place in the sky, this mirror flashes a beam of bright light down the long straight path and into the house, where it spotlights a statue standing in the hall.

We have seen how the most ancient gardens were designed philosophically, or – since in those early times there was little or no distinction – theologically. The most ancient of gardens were meant to reflect Paradise, the Garden of Eden, and in them a person could contemplate eternity and reflect on the greatest themes of humanity. The cloisters of monastic Europe took up this theme. Deep within the monastery, under the shadow of the chapel – the tallest and most glorious building of any religious house – monks and nuns designed for themselves gardens of reflection and meditation. Usually, the cloister ran on all four sides of a square of grass. The grass was sometimes broken by flowerbeds, and was often divided by paths that led to a central tree, well or statue. This was considered the shape and design most conducive to reflection.

Balanced against the extravagant and exhibitionist enterprises, the exotic and even erotic desires of the post-Renaissance, there has always been a design tradition that favoured the secret garden, the intimate and private place, the *hortus conclusus*, where gardeners can shut themselves away from the clamour of the world and meditate or philosophize in peace. Bacon praised his garden by saying that he 'found the situation of that place much convenient for the trial of my philosophical conclusions'. His model garden was laid out to provide shady walks, sitting places and private corners as well as banqueting halls, wide grass lawns and playful ornamental pools.

Although this notion was absorbed into the Landscape Movement of the 18th century and the formal bedding arrangements of the 19th century, it never disappeared. For example, from the 1740s William Shenstone laid out the land at The Leasowes, his grazing farm in Cheshire, deliberately to enhance thoughtful contemplation before the beauties of nature. He modelled his garden on Virgils' idealized agricultural estate in a style that became known as the *ferme ornée*. A walk around this garden provided the visitor with innumerable (we can still trace over 40 of them) viewing points, which, interestingly, were commonly called *reflecting* points. These offered seats, bowers, alcoves, screened benches and a root house – a structure made in the then fashionable 'rustic' style from misshapen tree roots. But more than that, many of these points offered highly designed and enclosed views, such as a narrow tree-shaded valley 'at once cool, gloomy, solemn and sequestered', and were decorated with engraved quotations to give their users something to think about, to reflect on. Henrietta, Lady Luxborough, a correspondent of Shenstone's, took such ideas a stage further: among the ornamentations of her garden she included a beehive in the library – a direct Virgilian reference and a provocative challenge to idleness.

In 1806 the young poet William Wordsworth proposed what must, in the full flower of the 'natural' or Romantic movement, have seemed an outrageous scheme: a tiny secluded garden, enclosed with trellis work containing not just box-edged flower borders but a central fountain as well. Wordsworth modelled

Opposite

George Carter, Raf Fulcher and Elizabeth Tate together created A Vision of Versailles for the 1984 Chelsea Flower Show. In this modern interpretation of one of Europe's great gardens, a central fountain, seen through an ornate portico, is reflected in a metal plate at the far end.

his proposed garden on one described in the 15th-century poem *The Flower and the Leaf* written by an anonymous woman poet under the influence of Chaucer. One of the explicit points about this poetic garden was that it was quite shut off from the outside world, 'the hegge as thik as a castle-wal', offering restful seating, like a 'pretty parlour' and secrecy, peace and solitude.

From the 1840s onwards, James Mellor designed a garden quite unlike any of his contemporaries. It was designed as a walk with a clear itinerary – a reflective stroll through the life of the Christian soul, with many of its features drawn from episodes in Bunyan's *Pilgrim's Progress*. You entered the domain through a Wicket Gate, and strolled past the Slough of Despond and Doubting Castle, together with other Christian symbols, memorials and artefacts, until you gained a distant view of the Delectable Mountains. Possibly in retaliation for this Protestant garden, the Vicar of Claydon in Sussex turned his garden into a *via dolorosa* – a replica of the journey taken by Christ to Calvary, the theme of all the Stations of the Cross that ornament churches and roadways in more Catholic countries.

Such explicitly religious, that is Christian, symbolism may no longer inspire many of us to the more general sort of reflection that these garden designs were aiming for. At the same time, as Anne Wareham has pointed out (see page 55), we lack detailed frames of reference in which classical, or other allusions can provoke us into contemplation.

Michael Shone's garden has a willow statue by Serena de la Haye in a wooded area; it shows an enchanting naked woman through a sun-dappled glade. In point of fact, it is a statue, made of woven willow lathes, of Daphne. Daphne was a nymph in classical mythology, who was pursued by the god Apollo. To escape his unwanted advances, she was turned into a laurel tree. The full appropriateness of her lathe-twisted naked presence in a wood, surrounded by laurel bushes, is lost on too many of us now. When Benini carved the same theme out of marble, he could be fairly certain that the story was sufficiently well known to his audience that they would recognize the subject and would be open to his interpretation of the myth. Today, classical statuary may give a garden *gravitas*, but much of its significance has been lost. A large hippopotamus wallowing in a muddy pool at the feet of an ascetic-looking medieval saint may raise a curious smile, but few will recognize the saint as Augustine, who was bishop of Hippo, in North Africa. Likewise, many people will not see the humour of putting a bust of the Emperor Hadrian in a wall.

The one area where this reflective element of garden design has become ubiquitous is the so-called Japanese garden. For some reason we have become culturally aware that Japanese gardening is contemplative, is 'spiritual', is Zen – which means calm and balance and serenity. Illustrations of classical Japanese gardens – three stones and a swirl of raked pebbles – leave us feeling that we do not really know what we are looking at or why; although some of the finest examples do indeed have an austere beauty of their own. On the whole, though, we are unconvinced by most of the Japanese-style gardens we have visited in the course of researching this book. Somehow, placing a Japanese lantern in what appears to be a child's sandbox brings on a mood of irritation rather than reflection. We suspect that the exact meaning of many of the clipped hedges, artificially placed rocks and tinkling bamboo wind chimes are not thought through, and are not deeply embedded in either culture or individual. It may well be the case that the vertical standing stones represent the 'Yang' or male principle, while horizontally laid ones represent 'Yin' or female values, but since we have no frame of reference to inform us, at the level of the eye or heart, what is meant to be learned from such references, this information is of little use to us and we cannot associate it with anything in our own lives. We may, of course, be lacking some sort of sensibility, but we are constantly unmoved by Japanese flourishes in the front garden of modern European houses.

These sorts of touches seem to work better when they are used wittily or even ironically – or when the Japanese mood is distilled from the Zen 'laws' of gardening. Thus, some of the most pleasing gardens

Opposite

Serena de la Haye's statue of Daphne moves towards you through the trees of the Shones' garden. The symbolism of the myth is all too often lost on us now, but the statue still manages to create a magical atmosphere.

The contemporary use of menhirs, obelisks and stone circles may be more aesthetic than mystical, but they can still bring a sense of the unknown to a garden. These evocative New Standing Stones are at The Garden House, Devon, in southwest England.

eschew the specificity of 'Japanese' or 'Chinese' and prefer the term 'oriental'. But the carefully positioned rocks at Hazlebury Manor in Wiltshire, where the architect Ian Pollard has created a grassy declivity that contains a circle of massive standing stones, speaks to me more clearly of ancient religious ideas and fits more organically into the structures and history of Salisbury Plain.

Maggie Keswick in her influential book on Chinese gardens taught a ready public that what was important was the business of relating the garden to the landscapes around it (by mirroring the distant mountains, for example, in the nearby artificial stone shapes). She showed how a minimalism and simplicity could hold single views completely still and perfectly calm for a moment. And how buildings, structures, distortions of plants, strong statements of the human and particularly symbolic statues and shapes could make people look again at the so-called natural. These seem lessons worth learning and interpreting into a genuinely local and contemporary idiom, instead of taking the objects themselves – be they *bonsai* plants, smiling Buddha statues, rattan fencing or raked sand – stripping them of their meaning and inserting them into improbable and unsuitable landscapes; or getting a book out of the library to design your garden after the abstracted and now culturally isolated 'laws' of *feng shui*. Just looking at a flight of steps, framed with bamboo and curving invitingly towards something out of sight, does more to demonstrate this wonderful magic – with the pure vertical lines of the bamboo emphasizing and shifting the light – than any imitation Japanese arrangement of clipped box to represent clipped azaleas or native British rock to represent oriental mountains. When combined with the strange rustling sound of the bamboo, the effect becomes irresistible. Following Maggie Keswick's suggestions, Peter Osborne's beech circle, oriented to frame and pull in the great peaks in the distance, has developed the Chinese notion of framing the distance in a truly local and authentic way.

Gardens for reflection and meditation need to be carefully thought out. In 1987, Raf Fulcher, Elizabeth Tate and George Carter created for the Chelsea Flower Show a garden designed in an entirely modern style to provoke such reflection. Their primary concern was to demonstrate the way in which light itself affected perception of garden structures, so they used high, solid wooden structures to divide the garden along two axes – one stressing the brightness and joy of the day, and the other the mystery and melancholy of the night. Where these axes crossed they placed an unusual fountain: a substantial glazed ball (representing the sun), mounted on a single post from which four jets of water emerged. Fulcher described the inspiration for the fountain as the 17th-century work of the hydraulic engineer Salomon de Caus and our old friend Thomas Bushell's imaginative labours at Enstone. However, although acknowledging that both these predecessors would have delighted in the possibilities that electricity would have given them, Fulcher's fountain had to be pumped manually, using an old-fashioned village hand pump. Fulcher explained this rather unexpected feature:

> Throwing a switch has become such an unthinking act that it wouldn't provoke a moment's contemplation. But if the gardeners are obliged to do the pumping for five minutes and sweat a bit, when they sit back to rest for twenty minutes and watch the jets cascading, it might make them think about what they have actually been doing and how they have harnessed natural phenomena to create an attractive effect; and once they begin to ponder on questions like that, goodness knows where their imaginations might take them. But it is certain that for a while they won't be preoccupied with more mundane matters and that should give them the sort of mental repose which all good gardens are supposed to offer.

This being the case it is slightly odd that the show garden fails to offer the energetic and reflective gardener anywhere *to sit*. None the less this is a provocative way of thinking about gardens, and one which shows how little we have actually learned from our studies of either our own garden history or reflection on the gardens of other cultures.

The idea of exertion followed by repose comes more readily to a contemporary gardener than it did to his or her 17th- and 18th-century ancestors, simply because they in all likelihood had servants to do the work, while they enjoyed the repose. There is less need now to force exertion on a gardener, although there remains a special sort of pleasure in relaxing after a sharp effort. A welcoming seat and a wide view at the top of a steep climb, for instance, offer a particular mode of reflection, but the effort of mowing the lawn or doing the weeding may be enough to make subsiding into a welcoming nook or corner force the brain into reflective or contemplative action.

Clearbeck, Peter Osborne's garden in Lancashire, which we have already mentioned, has a particular and highly personal atmosphere. It is essentially a landscaped garden that is open to the world and has wide views but within it there are a number of contained and enclosed inner gardens. At the centre of the garden is what Osborne calls his 'symbolic' garden, which was originally created as a place that was both sheltered from the prevailing strong winds and sunny; a place to sit and reflect. To aid that reflection this tiny inner enclosure has been designed with the greatest care. There is only one way into it – along a narrow walled path and through a pyramid. This approach is decorated with bones and planted with black and poisonous plants: the way into paradise is through death. For Osborne it is also through Christian baptism, so immediately on entering the garden you have to cross a small pond. And lest this should all seem a bit earnest, in the pond there is a clump of reeds and a ceramic basketweave pot planted with *Gypsophila* (Baby's Breath). It looks charming and appropriate – but the reference to the infant Moses in the bullrushes is there for the taking. Now you are in a paved courtyard with a bench at one end and some topiary balls growing in pots, while the sides of the garden are heavily planted. Again the references are not pressed: there are three topiary balls to represent the Trinity, though we discussed the possibility of growing three box balls on a single stem as a better representation of this theological entity.

As much for his amusement as anything else, all the plantings in this courtyard garden refer to angels or other theological imagery – for example, huge *Angelica arcangelica* were blooming magnificently when we were there. One would have to be extremely knowledgeable in plant names, both common and botanical, to pick all these references up of course, but held here in a moment of reflection at the heart of the garden, facing the improbable pyramid, your mind does start asking such questions. Without any theological interest at all you are lulled by the peace, the warmth and the protection from the wind and have the place and space seated on the stone bench and looking straight at the pyramid, to ask yourself, 'What is going on here?' 'Why?' But for the gardener himself the making of such tableaux requires more; it obliges him to think in a very disciplined manner about how and what to plant to reflect the underlying concept. Once the interior point of reference is established and brooded on, the actuality may move a long way from the starting point, but the whole design will remain rooted in something highly personal and solid. Gardening moves from a craft to an art form precisely when this sort of question is asked.

A garden is for many things. In design terms, it has complex functions, but historically we can learn that just 'being pretty' is a beginning not an end: gardens can also be funny, or clever or, as we have been discussing here, thought-provoking, contemplative, reflective. It is these elements that elevate a garden from the ordinary to the special. We need to reflect more on our gardens themselves – what we want them to do and be. If we seriously think of them as art, an expression of our human creativity, then they must reflect our whole personalities, not just our ability to practise horticultural techniques, which are surely a means to an end rather than the project itself.

Opposite

The most sheltered area in the garden at Clearbeck invites rest and reflection. Designed with the greatest care, this tiny enclosure is full of meaning for its creator. Whether you understand the symbolism or not doesn't matter – the atmosphere of the place removes you from the rest of the garden and demands that you ask questions of it.

5

Sacred Groves and Magic Forests

Philosophy is odious and obscure.
Both law and physic are for petty wits.
Divinity is basest of the three,
Unpleasant, harsh, contemptible and vile.
'Tis magic, magic that hath ravished me.

CHRISTOPHER MARLOWE, *The Tragical History of Dr Faustus* (1604)

WHITEHURST, JOHN AND LYNN MERCY'S 0.6-hectare (1½-acre) garden in Kent, greets the visitor in a fairly conventional way with a large lawn surrounded by borders and trees. Except … a white-painted Victorian wrought iron spiral staircase leads from the lawn up into a tree, in summer its upper reaches invisible in the green leaves. Just as a visual effect it is somehow heart-stopping but it invites you to climb it, and when you do there is a walkway leading both through the heart of large trees and hedges on stilts and along the very tops of apple trees. It zig-zags, giving the impression of being longer than it is. It creates a magical world of its own; the stuff of children's dreams made real.

Elsewhere in the garden the Mercys pull the same magical surprises in various different ways. Unseen from the house there are a series of ponds. When the great willow tree that grew beside one of them fell across the stream, they left it to form a living bridge. Today, fresh branches have sprung up from the fallen trunk to create a new set of vertical lines, so you cross the water within the tree and descend the other side by steps that have been integrated by extending the old tree trunk to the ground.

Traditionally, grape vines grown in hot houses in Britain had their roots outside the walls to suit their horticultural needs; then a hole was drilled through the wall and the main stem brought inside so that they would receive enough heat for the bunches of grapes to ripen. The Mercys have taken this process one stage further: their vine has its roots against the wall of the house, but its branches have been taken into the otherwise fairly conventional drawing room and trained along walls. (Alas it does not bear fruit inside, but the effect is once again unexpected, mysterious and fantastic.)

Currently, they are completing a mound: a traditional form favoured throughout the 17th century and adopted by neo-classicists in the 18th century. The Mercys' mound is different, however; it contains a room – a cross between a grotto and a children's play house. The room has a little wood-burning stove in it, and the chimney is taken up inside the structure. When it is working, smoke will puff out of the mound, which will resemble a sleepy volcano or a sleeping dragon.

Opposite
The Mercys' aerial walkway transports visitors into a magical space above the garden. In this way a fresh and childlike perspective is created.

With a similar spirit, the Mercys collect their bath water in a tank on top of a pergola, level with the first floor of their house. Water pressure alone – the old hydraulic engineering effect so loved by de Caus and Bushell – carries the water down a pipe and under the lawn, where it is then forced up again to moisten the thin and exposed soil of a meadow on the roof of a shed.

These features help to create an atmosphere that is part dreamlike, part childlike (not childish); there is something enchanted about the Mercys' garden. Although their children grew up at Whitehurst, they only began to develop the garden after John Mercy had recovered from a serious stroke. We hope it is not intrusive to wonder if it is this very fact – being so near to death – that gives his imagination its wonderfully magical turn. A time and a place for reflection after danger might indeed help to bring on such an approach to gardening in the right person.

Another 'interpretation' of Whitehurst's inspiration is rather different. The hydraulic watering system, the keeping and utilizing of the crippled willow tree, the openness to magic itself might arise from an instinctive ecological sensitivity; an awareness of participation in the process of life and growth rather than the consciousness of the division between nature and art which appears to lie behind some of the wittiest and most reflective gardens.

This is speculation, but it is speculation with some basis. Another garden that impels the use of the word 'magical' belongs to David Rosewarne – an artist and garden designer who is very aware of the ecological aspects and implications of gardening. Despite the fact that his garden is urban – it is located in Ealing in West London – it has an extraordinary atmosphere of magic. Rosewarne's principles are highly organic, but the garden hasn't been 'left to nature' – the whole thing is deeply thought through, and more atavistic than artistic. Rosewarne himself uses the language of religion: 'the garden is my church – I am its priest.' But this does not for him imply 'letting things happen' – it means making things happen. One of his rules is that *nothing* gets thrown away: in a previous garden he burned all the naturally generated garden rubbish, and subsequently tried a shredder, which proved too noisy to be pleasing; now he 'recycles', but in a highly artful manner.

At the centre of the garden is a huge weeping willow tree. It shades the garden, but also dissipates light through its branches, which are seldom still. Willow trees shed a great deal – not only leaves but also the long stalks that carry the leaves. These sheddings have been piled up around the trunk of the tree to form an ever-elaborating triple structure. There is a bower – a bench entirely roofed by branches and twigs – where you can sit looking away from the house, deeper into the garden. There is also a cave, with a tiny narrow entrance leading to a den that has windows and seats. Although this was nominally created for Rosewarne's son, David admitted that children like to build their own dens, and that this is really his lair. The third aspect of the mound is a statue; a huge and mysterious face of an ancient willow god, the Green Man of English tradition. One of his eyes is also a window for the den, and the other opens through into the bower. At the humorous level Rosewarne calls the structure a 'twigloo'; at another, equally true, level it is the presiding genius of his garden.

In the afternoon, from the bowered seat built into the twigloo, the far end of the garden looks like a woodland glade. One of the strange effects of this garden is that although it is really quite small – approximately 30 x 15 metres (100 x 50 feet) – and entirely surrounded first by a wall and then by other houses, and despite the fact that there are only a few trees, albeit mature ones, rising high above the other planting, it can be reasonably described as a 'woodland garden'. Rosewarne has abandoned lawn in favour of underplanting. Wide paths, apparently laid casually, and constructed of 'left overs' – paving brick or gravel – appear to roam along the topographic contours of the space, creating a sense of level and diversity. There is a 'dell', a terrace with a fountain, a vegetable patch and a gazebo or arbour, but it does not *feel*

Right
David Rosewarne's deep belief in recycling garden 'waste' has helped to create a garden with an extraordinary atmosphere. Here, the summerhouse and its surroundings are clothed in scrap that both contrasts and blends in a magical way with the garden's plants.

Left
The Mythic Garden at Stone Farm houses an ever-changing display of artworks amid the national collection of birch and alder trees. Placing the pieces is also an art — here, Dinosaur *by Bridget Arnold nestles in the ground like a giant egg ready to hatch.*

like an ordinary garden. The space is divided by screens, which are once again woven out of the garden's own detritus: the inspiration for this weaving came from the Christmas wreaths that the citizens of the historic township of Williamsburg in the USA make for their doorways at Christmas time. Here they are constructed out of last year's flower heads, old twigs, anything that comes to hand. Some of them frame peep-holes, some of them decorate the backs of garden seats. Most are left where they grew as long as possible – when we visited the garden in late April the cardoon seed-heads from the summer before were still in place on their now freshly sprouting and re-greened plants. No doubt when they fall over they will be moved somewhere else.

Even the shards of pottery and old ceramics that have been dug up in the course of constructing this garden are displayed, lining the windows of the summerhouse, balanced with great care at the bottom of each pane of glass – some of them tiny, but each respectfully mounted: it is not just nature but history that is being celebrated. But just when you think you are beginning to 'understand something about the Natural Principle' or 'true organics' you are surprised. In the potager, and indeed in the 'wilder' area under the trees, there are brilliantly coloured chard stalks – a vivid and totally unnatural yellow, along with oranges and reds: American hybrids, useful vegetables and garish ornament simultaneously.

David Rosewarne's accuracy of eye and hand – perhaps unsurprisingly he is a professional artist – mean that he can pull off this highly contrived informality. The excellence of execution gives real freedom, but so does a real belief in the sacred, which is reflected not only in the structures and ornamentation but also in the delight in skilful planting, in co-operating with or even 'serving' the natural process through intervention and attention, which manifests itself in organic techniques and ecological awareness as much as it does in delightfully eccentric features.

On the northeastern corner of Exmoor, down narrow lanes with high hedges that cut out the long views of the rising moorland, Kenneth and June Ashburner have created the 'Mythic Garden' at Stone Farm. Across a 2.4-hectare (6-acre) sloping site they have arranged the National Collection of birch and alders into a garden; each variety, grown from seed, is planted into small groves, with the ground beneath them kept clear and grass paths running between and around them. The slender and often highly coloured trunks, rising like pillars or columns, create an atmosphere almost like a cathedral or ancient temple, while the delicate leaves above let through a dappled sunlight. In addition to the trees themselves, a good deal of gardening has been done – although the garden appears pure, simple and almost untended, in reality some clever planting breaks up the wood with occasional patches of colour or undergrowth, and at the lower end pools have been dug. There is also an Art Gallery: each year a collection of works, mainly by local artists and in the spirit of a natural mythology, are displayed throughout the garden. A slightly dangerous-looking Pan figure rises from the water in one pond; a highly abstract *chaise-longe* of metal and moss invites one deeper into a grove; faces, abstract shapes and a sweeping weaving hanging from a branch help to create an atmosphere of peace, and strange magic.

There are very few specific points that link Whitehurst, Rosewarne's garden and Stone Farm, except a willingness to follow one's own instinct and a love of what one is doing that overrides fashion, common sense or even social embarrassment. To accept that human skills – art and artistry and amusement – are a part of nature requires a kind of bold humility that has traditionally been a mark of the holy. Probably you cannot teach people to make magical gardens – they have to flow spontaneously from the inner self of the gardener – although this is true of all good gardens.

None the less, without perhaps being able to define what one means very precisely, there are gardens, or parts of larger gardens, that are 'magical'. They bring out a response in their visitors which is somehow childlike – a mixture of awe and delight. They make you feel small but happy to be so. Although they may be very unusual, the word 'eccentric' is not appropriate: etymologically, eccentric means 'away from or out of the centre', and truly magical gardens are the exact opposite – they give you a sense of being nearer the centre than usual, whatever that centre is. It is easier to identify magical gardens than it is to classify the features and elements that make them magical.

There are a few historical gardens that have always been recognized as magical in this sense. They often sit awkwardly in books on the history of gardening, because it is singularly difficult to slot them neatly into the usual fashion-and-development pattern that such histories must follow: they also seem to decay and therefore disappear swiftly – as though they had to be the inspiration of an individual or a specific site and time. Here we are going to mention only three such gardens: the Sacro Bosco at Bomarzo in Marche, Italy, from the Renaissance; Hermann Furst von Puckler-Muskau's 19th-century traveller's garden at Branitz Park in Germany; and the 13th-century garden of the Saiho-ji Temple in Kyoto, Japan.

We have already mentioned the garden at Bomarzo. It is especially curious because we know so much about Italian gardens of a similar period and yet the experts cannot quite establish a frame of reference for it, even though it shares with its contemporaries certain features such as extravagant statuary. But instead of confining the grotesque to an occasional grotto or particular glade the whole garden is shaped by bizarre almost out-of-scale monumental carvings set apparently randomly in a wooded area. No one has really succeeded in working out the intention or symbolic meaning of this Sacred Grove, although one has to believe there was one: the scale and scope of the whole thing is too extreme for it to have been merely a whim. The fact that the Sacred Grove has fallen into decay actually enhances its spell-binding qualities. Once there were wild things, gods or monsters, in these woods, and then they were frozen forever. Was it a magic spell, a punishing curse, or a love of the green place where they found themselves?

We know more about Branitz Park – von Puckler-Muskau designed it to reflect his worldwide wanderings. Here, he brought together his own synthesis of East and West, and his own mixing of architectural and landscape styles, to create a series of islands that float on a lake, and dark woods that are punctuated by mysterious artefacts and structures.

The moss garden at the Saiho-ji Temple is the oldest of these gardens – more than 800 years have gone into the landscape. The lake here is carved into the shape of the Japanese pictogram for life itself, and the curious monotony of ancient vertical trees and low-lying moss plants creates an atmosphere that is almost too strange to be pleasing.

None of these gardens could be satisfactorily copied today; but it is worth looking at what they do have in common, and considering how, if this is an effect you would like to achieve, they could be referred to or 'quoted'. When we visited the Monster Walk, created by the late Michael Shone at White's Farmhouse in Oxfordshire, it reminded us of Bomarzo. When we said this to his family they laughed and acknowledged that this had indeed been his direct inspiration. One side of this garden drops very sharply down a slope so steep that it is almost a cliff to a river below. The river here was once a watercress farm, and was consequently channelled into minor floods. The watercress still grows there, a vivid green mat at the foot of the slope that is effectively not cultivable. Michael Shone cut a zig-zagging path down through the vegetation, which he left predominantly to its own devices. And then, half hidden in the undergrowth, he introduced 'monsters': a suspended pterodactyl flaps over head, a giant tortoise lurks beneath your feet, there are crocodiles and other undefined creatures half hidden. When it reaches the bottom the path crosses and recrosses the river and runs on a causeway through the bright green underwater cress meadow. Here a plastic inflatable whale wallows, and when you tread on a pressure pad on the path nearby it spouts water and moans loudly.

Although Shone's Monster Walk is delightfully funny, it is more than that – it has a sort of elemental feeling about it. It is neither garden nor wilderness; it is excessively almost unnaturally green, but at the same time overgrown and tangled. The idea that monsters are lying in wait gives a feeling of strangeness that counterbalances the simply amusing, and weights it towards the magical.

On the whole, magical gardens do not draw their inspiration from historic gardens, but from other cultural dimensions altogether: from the mythical, the legendary; from fairy stories, folk tales and the twilight of pre-history. Rosewarne's Green Man is part of a folk tradition still kept alive in the Neolithic sites that dot parts of our countryside almost casually.

There is a vogue for a rather ill-defined Celtic spirituality at present, which is sometimes misplaced, but can work well in gardens if it slots into a shared sense of landscape. There are lots of people who cannot, as we pointed out earlier in the book, access classical allusions to trigger a reflective sensibility, but who remain touched, moved and elevated by, for example, labyrinths. They may not know anything at all about their origins or purposes, but they sense something is there – some magical movement. Although this can terribly easily collapse into the easily sentimental or the self-righteous, it can also be brought to bear as a frame of reference in a garden in ways that are quite unexpected, and sometimes even otherworldly.

History itself is unclear about the origins and meanings of much of the pre-historic record in Britain: what is clear is that we have one. Along with the stone circles (and in Norfolk the wood circle recently uncovered in the shifting sands of the coastline) and standing stones, there are the chalk figures carved into the hillsides of the South West, the massive earthworks of Silbury Hill and its surroundings and the roadways that cut across the South Downs. These blend seamlessly into remnants of Celtic culture – the mysteries of Glastonbury, the ancient hermitages, shrines and holy wells of Wales, grass mazes and pathways, place names, traces of Arthurian legend, Holy Island and Iona. With an odd lack of historic sense, almost everything that is not Roman but is pre-Norman conquest is touched with an aura of magic. These relics have an atmosphere of loneliness, of beauty and of greenness; the mood caught by, for example, some of Dylan Thomas's poetry: 'The force that through the green fuse drives the flower, drives my green age.' A collection of deep-set, if unspecified, references that are highly interpretable in garden design terms.

In the 1980s Ian Pollard, an architect, began to develop his garden at Hazelbury Manor in Wiltshire on 73 hectares (180 acres) of farmland. Although on an entirely different scale, he utilized a similar approach to the Mercys. Around the Tudor manor house are a series of basically conventional gardens, which are broadly formal in structure, using topiary, lawn, herbaceous and annual planting, paved terraces walks and steps. There is a traditional walled kitchen garden and a wide application of urns and statuary and the other appurtenances of the English country garden. But beyond the formal gardens the mood changes abruptly: the walker comes quite suddenly upon a grassy declivity and within it is a stone circle – massive local rocks laid out as they are at Avebury. Beyond them are two tumuli – earthworks reflecting the Wiltshire downs beyond. Spiral pathways coil around them, and a turf labyrinth is laid out on the rising ground. In this same area Ian Pollard is now adding a topiary Stonehenge. These are not 'fakes' – as indeed the topiary makes clear – and they are not religious sites. This is landscape gardening with a new feel – instead of 18th-century Italianisms, Ian Pollard has gone back to the roots of the land and the result, especially after the beautifully artificial 'proper' gardens nearer the house, is magical.

At the Garden House, Buckland Monochorum in Devon, a single huge dolmen has been placed at the end of a rising vista: the effect is remarkably different from the one that a classical statue or other object would produce. This seems to me an interesting example of how our eyes do not ever work independently of our memories and other cultural associations. An obelisk, for example, would fill the space in the same way and would, in terms of its geometry, be a very similar shape – vertical, solid, tapering. An Italian cypress would also provide the same outline. Yet, even at a distance each of these objects would produce very different emotional reactions.

Scaled right down to suit a small cottage, the potter Andy Gill, with design assistance from Dan Pearson, has constructed his Gloucestershire garden with direct reference to the Rollwright Stones – another group of standing stones which are, as the Wiltshire Downs are to Hazelbury, local to him.

A less direct quotation from these sorts of ancient and mysterious prehistoric works has been laid out in a tiny narrow back garden in Birmingham. Here, Candy Diamond has laid out the paved path that runs alongside the typical extension at the back of her terraced house in the shape of a dragon or lizard. It sprawls there, converting a perfectly ordinary back garden into a magical lair. Part of the magic is that you could walk over it repeatedly without consciously seeing the shape, although from any point of elevation, such as a first-floor window, it is absolutely and inescapably present.

Perhaps the most utilized of these ancient effects, and one that can be reproduced fairly simply, is the turf maze. Jane Sutherland, who is designing the Millennium Maze in Market Bosworth, Leicestershire (a collective project involving the Tree Council, the local authority and David Bellamy's Conservation Foundation among others), explained to me the difference between the two sorts of mazes. Celtic mazes, which she prefers to call labyrinths, are to be walked; they are about a physical process, a journey or pilgrimage. Normally they are laid out flat on the ground, most often by simply mowing the grass where the path is, although they can be paved. By following the path you can walk in and walk out again: the contentment is in the *doing*. Classical mazes are an intellectual challenge; you have to find the centre which is hidden – either visually by high walls, traditionally clipped hedges – or by some tricky devise which you have to solve. The satisfaction is on reaching the middle and discovering what is hidden there, in *solving* the problem. Predominantly Celtic labyrinths are spiral, with no straight lines, while mazes are traditionally rectilinear. Labyrinths are magical; mazes are human and intellectual. Jane Sutherland goes further and believes that labyrinths follow a 'female' principle while mazes are 'masculine' in their inspiration.

Although obviously there are mazes that cross between these two types, and those that present different atmospheres altogether, this seems, judging by the gardens in which we have located them, to be a generally sound guiding principle. We will look at classical mazes and their modern descendants more in the next chapter; here it is worth observing that, especially at dawn and dusk when the effect of the variation in shadow emphasizes the difference between the mown and the unmown grass, spiralled labyrinths do have a strange aura, and bring on an almost eerie feeling. They can be located on their own and encountered by surprise, in a woodland glade or a sunken garden. Equally, as at Hazelbury or Kay Buxton's labyrinth in Norfolk, they can be placed on the side of a hill so that their strange shape can enchant and invite participation from a distance.

Certain earthworks, or what is now commonly called Land Art, refer, like the maze paths, back to the Celtic and Neolithic traditions: tumuli can be as magical as mounds can be formal. The earth-carved sea in Janis Hall's Waterland Garden in Connecticut or, albeit in a more obviously contemporary idiom, Maya Lin's 'Wave Field' at the University of Michigan both draw their strength from their association with the most ancient traditions, while James Pierce in Maine or Charles Jencks in Dumfries and Galloway have consciously drawn on the old shapes of burial mounds and grass ramparts and the hill forts of the English Downs in shaping their landscapes so magically.

Above

Labyrinths are imbued with meaning; they are mystical symbols of life's journey or sacred reflections of the universe. This simple example created by Jessica Duncan has a central stone carved with the following words by T.S. Eliot: 'The still point in a turning world'.

The points of reference in these gardens are fairly easily identified and described, even though it is often difficult to capture why they offer the sort of emotional reward that they do. But there is another sort of magical garden whose intellectual framework is harder to locate. Often these gardens seem to crystallize elements of a fairy story – a combination of romance and wonder, a touch of the Gothic, of Germanic fantasy or even of dream. In several cases we have found it well nigh impossible to be certain whether a particular garden feature *really* belongs in this chapter or in the earlier chapter on laughter and humour or, of course, in both. In the end it comes down to the overall atmosphere of a garden rather than the feature itself. Where and how something is placed in a garden creates the mood in which it is seen.

It would be tidy, for instance, to argue that while gazebos and follies – note their very name – belonged in a tradition of wit and self-consciousness, summerhouses, pavilions, arbours, caves and grottoes were primarily magical. Unfortunately, the names themselves are rather vaguely applied: on many occasions the name gardeners choose for their built structures may reflect, deliberately or otherwise, their understanding of what they are doing more generally. Why exactly is Sue Prideaux's folly (see page 75) a folly not a summerhouse? The answer is probably that her garden makes continual reference to the 18th-century landscape tradition and 'follies' were what such gardens had. There may be more complex answers

too: her folly sits high and 'naked' above its lakes; it is to be looked up at as much as to be looked out from;
it is exposed, not secret.

Why did we call the tower at Corpusty Mill a folly and place it in the chapter on wit, despite the fact
that it is romantic and 'medieval' and reminiscent in so many ways of childhood fantasies, while Michael
Shone's castle tower at White's Farmhouse, despite the fact that it is made of wooden poles and makes no
claim to historicity at all, is about to be described here? Both towers have staircases and viewing platforms
at the top, but from Corpusty Mill you look over the clear and precise garden wall on to an ordinary
village green – the tower emphasizes the privacy of the garden, the stand it is making against the mundane
– from the tower at White's Farmhouse you look out only on the garden– the tower draws attention to
the kingdom of the gardener. And the gardens themselves are very different. You approach the Corpusty
Mill folly across a beautifully mown lawn with a highly contrived and exotically planted water garden
around you. You approach the White's Farmhouse tower through a (tiny) 'wild' woodland where you have
already encountered a willow statue; the tower is surrounded by shaggy shrubbery cut through with tiny
paths and little tunnels – you come upon it after a hard journey, and you have to cross a miniature

Opposite

Follies that seem to spring from the pages of a fairy tale still have the power to fill us with wonder, particularly when, as here, they form part of a frozen landscape.

Right

Constructed in 1981 by Sir Frederick Gibberd for his grandchildren, this moated castle is truly magical. A working drawbridge, ramparts and a flagpole enchant children and adults alike.

drawbridge to get in. Although both towers are in fact intellectually complex in their frames of reference, the sophistication at White's Farmhouse is in the way that it disguises itself while at Corpusty Mill it proclaims itself.

The moated castle in the Gibberd Garden in Essex is also magical. Although the garden contains many works of art, you are continually surprised and delighted by its many childlike touches, which include a tree-house and other feaures as well as the moated castle. It is not so much about sophisticated wit but childlike delight.

Perhaps a clearer contrast can be made with summerhouses. At the Menagerie in Northamptonshire the two summerhouses are, from the outside, four summerhouses. That is to say that, since their fronts and backs are completely different – a witty concept in itself – there appear to be four different summerhouses. Two of these façades face out on to formal intricate plantings; their style – one classical and one Gothic – is referential and they function as the closing point of well-designed vistas. They are follies, deliberate jokes. On the other side, however, the same buildings are rustic, and they both look out on water gardens – one a native wetland garden and the other an exotic bog garden. They are not set up to be viewed from a distance, but to be discovered like Hansel and Gretel's gingerbread house in the woods; you see them across the water, through reeds, half hidden in planting; or you look out from them onto the water and the pretending wildness. They are magical pavilions.

In the end a sense of magic in a garden seems to come down to something as nebulous as 'atmosphere', something not clearly definable even when it is clearly present. None the less, we have noticed some elements that are common to many of the gardens that have enchanted us and that are somehow more conducive to this magical atmosphere than others.

One is a slight air of neglect. The garden in Frances Hodgson Burnett's *The Secret Garden* sounds very like a truly magical garden in the sense that we are trying to use it here. It has a mysterious decay, a lack of perfect lines; it is a little overgrown – as though the people who loved and made the garden have gone away for a while. And with the neglect comes a certain solitariness. Ideally, unless the house perfectly matches the intended mood of magic, the garden should be a little distant from it, or screened in some way. Likewise the edges of the garden should not be too sharply defined.

Trees are very important. In several of the gardens we have described in this chapter willow trees play an important part. We think this is not entirely coincidence. A mature willow tree always looks slightly distorted and strange, while the way that it breaks up sunshine without entirely closing it off can be both mysterious and bright at the same time. Beech and horse-chestnut trees in the early spring, with the almost incredible translucence of their bright green leaves, are also effective in this way. Perhaps the most reliably magical effect is of a clearing within a wood, ideally a wood of native (or native appearing) trees; especially those with silver trunks such as birches. Multi-trunked birch trees in a grove, with little or nothing growing under them, can send shivers up the spine of the most unromantic of people, as the magical groves at Stone Farm demonstrate.

A glade or island that is discovered unexpectedly in a wilder setting is one of the most reliable ways to produce the mood we are describing here. Surprisingly often, however, such a feature will contain something completely 'human', unnatural, blatantly contrived, such as a statue, building, fountain, pool or unexpected planting. This is one of the enchantments of Ian Hamilton Finlay's garden (see pages 119–23); or of the little boathouse under trees beside the lake at Peter Osborne's Clearbeck: they create a constant movement of the eye and mind between 'wilderness' and 'art', between nature and culture. Perhaps this is a throwback to the fairy stories of infancy, where the lost or abandoned child wanders through the scary forest and suddenly comes on an inhabited glade – a sugar-candy house, a sleeping

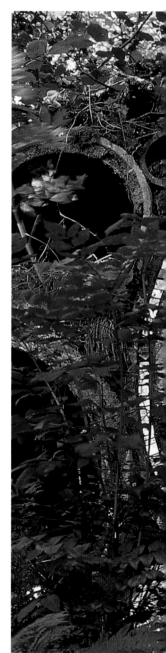

Below
The simplest materials can bring a bit of magic to a garden. Ivan Hicks's mystic pool, seen in the Enchanted Forest in Kent, is made from pieces of pipe and mirror.

maiden, a castle or a garden. This can work on quite a small scale: a seat or a table and chair in a 'neglected' orchard, an area of mown grass in a wild-flower meadow, even – as Anne Wareham's garden shows – an enamel plaque pinned to the trunk of a tree, force the questions, 'Who has been here?' 'Am I alone?' 'What is the 'wild wood?' and 'What is the garden?' When these human markers have more obvious mythical or legendary content this sensation can be intensified. Peter Randall-Page's heavy seedpod sculpture, *Granite Song,* on its tiny island, or Peter Osborne's monolith-sundial, with its precisely scored 'clock' of burned lines in the grass below it both draw on our already-present narrative of the fairy world to provide a framework beyond the simply pretty or charming.

Tiny curved paths through meadow or wood, especially mown grass ones, can also invite the visitor into a magical world. This is particularly true if they lead, or seem to lead *somewhere*. Paths that have to be negotiated; paths where the walker has to push their way through or under or round obstacles; tunnels of greenery, or long grasses that appear to impede the passer-by; a sense that around this corner all efforts will be rewarded by something, something special – this is the stuff of enchantment. Is this the prince of our lost dreams searching out the sleeping maiden? Paths that change level are particularly potent; grassed steps or even stairways cut into the land lead the walker *inwards,* as much as upwards or downwards. Moreover, as the Mercys' garden suggests, there is something beguiling about seeing a garden from different, and especially from unusual, angles – being high in the trees, or enclosed in a deep dell; being invited to look upwards along a view which later is seen downwards from the other end. The path through the tree-tops at Whitehurst has a fairy tale feeling about it, precisely because we do not often see the garden from the trees' point of view. Although they do not offer quite the same sense of movement, tree houses or even simpler platforms high above the ground, held in the safety of enormous branches and rocking slightly like a ship at sea, also delight and entrance. But so do caves, sunken gardens, and seating places behind and within waterfalls.

Movement of air or water also enhances this sense of being in a magical place. Like many of the effects that we have been describing here, they are usually most effective on the small scale. The effect of wind – again not of wilder storms but of the movement of air, the rustle of breezes, the ripple across water or through long grasses – touches some usually buried part of many people's imaginations. It might seem that wind effects present gardeners with particular difficulties because they are so hard to control or manage – and perhaps that is part of their charm: while the sound of water and its reflective qualities can be planned for in advance, the wind – like the Spirit – 'bloweth where it listeth', and even the most dedicated gardeners must take what they are given. As a matter of fact, modern technology can deliver a convincing ripple effect on a sheet of water, or even a steady and well-directed breeze if required; but even without going to these lengths there are a number of devices or schemes that will manipulate even the movement of air.

Everyone is aware that some parts of a garden are more sheltered than others, and that these can be shifted and changed by careful planning of wind breaks and wind tunnels. There are also particular plants that 'perform' especially well in even the lightest breeze. Most famously, the leaves of aspen trees are hung on twisted stalks – an evolutionary development to suit them for survival in very dry and windy environments. Each leaf will turn sideways to the wind, thus protecting the moisture and the fabric of their flat surfaces. From the gardener's point of view, however, this means that they will quiver and dance constantly in any movement of air. Trees with leaves that are differently coloured on their two sides – such as poplars, *Magnolia grandiflora* or some *Sorbus*'s – also appear to be more alive to the wind, the alternating shades creating a strong visual sense of movement. Reeds and grasses, especially those with loose seed heads, are very sensitive to movements in the air, as anyone who has seen the wind travelling across a cornfield is aware. Pampas grasses swaying in a light breeze or bowing before a stiffer wind create a sensation both of the sea and of the pampas itself heavy with wheat or oats; the effect is enhanced if they – or other wind-moving plantings – can be seen through or over far more stable forms, such as solid clipped hedges, stone walls, metal grilles or 'rigid' statuary. Bamboos are not only easily moved, they also, as we discussed earlier, make the most wonderful rustly music as they move, almost like water itself.

There are, additionally or alternatively, cultural artefacts that draw attention to the movement of the wind. Above all the subtle dancing of wind vanes make visible the invisible element of air. Wind vanes

Right
Geoffrey Stinton has solved the age-old problem of a durable Aeolian harp by using modern glass fibre resins. The science in each design is distinctly magical and seemingly unpredictable. However, over 30 years he has produced instruments that are both musical and beautiful in themselves.

have a long tradition. The cockerel on the church spire – spinning above the great stability of the architecture, heralding the dawn, surveying the landscape and informing the community of the day's weather – is a symbol of hope, change and possibility. There is a vast range of designs of wind vane now available; but they are not always deployed in the most imaginative or creative ways. They can speak very directly of the interests and imagination of their owner; taking up their ancient symbolic role in a modern form. They do not have to be restricted to roof tops, but can be incorporated into garden design, as art works, somewhere between science and fantasy, between information and magic. The gold dragon apparently dancing to the music of the wind chimes suspended under it on the peak of Craig Wincoll's

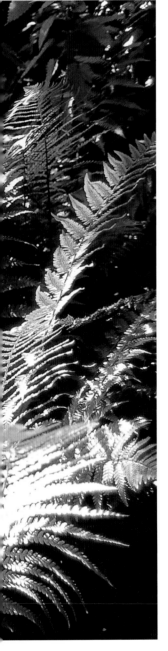

pergola at the Porter's Lodge is an artificial effect that is entirely in keeping with the garden. Equally harmonious, the gaunt wings or sails of Andrew Kray's iron wind vanes moving above the 'natural' wild planting around Peter Osborne's lake at Clearbeck draw attention to the continual effect of the wind over both water and plantings. They move themselves with great sensitivity, contrasting nature and artifice, as well as being beautiful objects in their own right.

Not all reminders of this fourth element, the magical air – which is, with the other elements, the source and sustenance of life, and of gardens – have to be visual. The wind across certain plants liberates their scent, and wind can be encouraged to make music. Very simple and easily constructed, wind chimes, well placed and well executed, remind us aurally that the wind is blowing and the air is never still. Different materials – metal, wood, stone, plastic – have very different qualities of sound, and it is worth going to considerable efforts to decide what atmosphere different tones encourage within the context of one's own garden and one's own memory bank.

Just as modern technology has allowed the return of the water organ to the Porter's Lodge, it has also permitted the redevelopment of the Aeolian harp. Named after Aeolus, the Greek god of the winds, Aeolian harps were 17th-century instruments designed to catch the wind and convert it into music. They were often built of wood, with strings like a violin or similar instrument, and placed for example within a window frame, so that the wind could 'bow' the strings, causing them to vibrate. The sound was then enhanced in a sound box behind the strings. Unfortunately they never worked very well; any material stable enough to keep the strings permanently tight lacked resonating qualities, while wood – which resonates wonderfully – tended to warp and move in the open air. Glass fibre resins have solved that problem – Geoffrey Stinton in West Sussex has been working on the technology and form of contemporary Aeolian harps for nearly 30 years. The 'science' is immensely tricky and, he told us, distinctly magical; he has constructed harps with elaborate care, which then refuse to play a single note. The idea was there and clearly possible but the results were for a long time elusive, which probably adds to the effectiveness of his discoveries. On a gentle slope of a not particularly exposed garden on a very calm and sunny day we heard the moaning music of the wind, harnessed through the old gods and ultra-modern materials and technology. Geoffrey Stinton was commissioned to build a harp to be placed on a beach in Cornwall, where its shell-shaped and somehow organic appearance is entirely appropriate, and where the wind blows across it freely.

These Aeolian harps are almost a symbol of what it is that we are arguing for in this book: an entirely contemporary expression of a traditional garden concept. They are beautiful in themselves and go way beyond the present dominance of blooming flowers in garden design. They bring together science and mythology, nature and culture; and they make one think – about what is natural and what is art, what is human and what is wild. They are, in this sense, witty, while at the same time the way that they look and the sounds that they make are lovely, strange and magical.

One of the reasons they are so effective is because they are, in every sense of the word, art. Their form maybe organic, but they never 'pretend' to be natural or 'found' objects. At present we seem to have a cultural tendency to associate 'high art' with grand gardens in the formal style, and *objets trouvés*, craftwork or 'charm' with natural or romantic gardens. In particular, we often do not seem to enjoy making the mental effort required to see and appreciate contemporary, particularly abstract or semi-abstract art forms, true modern sculpture in a so-called natural setting.

This need not be the case. Indeed, quite the reverse. Obviously the precise piece of statuary has to be chosen and placed with great care in relation to the whole garden. This is what often goes wrong with the so-called sculpture parks and gardens, which need to have changing exhibitions and cultural commitments other than those of a garden, so that too often they end up with a museum-effect without the convenience of a roof. But if the whole idea of the garden is kept in mind, with its frames of reference and its overall feel, the unexpected presence of a major artwork does more than give a small jolt to the viewer. Anyone who has seen the Henry Moore sculptures scattered on the hills above Springholm in Galloway, for instance, has experienced the way in which art of the right style for the place can actually make you see the place better. With the Henry Moores, the massive curves and weightiness do reflect the hills around, do make you realize how firmly they are founded and how immovable they appear to be: they take on a new sinuosity, because the art makes you think about sinuosity and density. At Grizedale in the Lake District the entirely contemporary sculptures that are apparently dotted randomly about the forest completely confuse one's vision: before long one is looking at the most 'natural' of objects – stones by the path and the shapes of branches, asking oneself if they, too, are 'art'. While sometimes the effect of art in gardens can be genuinely provocative, challenging one to question the art/nature split, sometimes they can just add to an atmosphere of magic.

These sorts of art work their effect in part by challenging the natural, but also by challenging our ideas about time. Do trees or marble statues last longer? What was here first, the earth or the person who so shaped it? Statuary stays still, stays fixed, while nature rambles around it, and changes with the seasons as well as with the longer reaches of the years. Great art lays claims on the infinite, and that in a garden can be its magic.

But the reverse, the fleeting, the deliberately temporary can have the same effect. Although we usually imagine that gardens will refer us to the long term, the slow revolution of seasons and planets, the harmony of the spheres, the everlasting calm of paradise, they can equally offer the magic of the ephemeral, the vanishing, the 'only today'. There are 'natural' effects that flood a garden with this sort of magic, such as the summer solstice, which we are culturally able to see and experience as enchanting. Similarly, ice and snow can be planned for and change the face of a garden. There are several books on 'the garden in winter' which depend almost entirely on effects that gardeners either cannot design or have made no effort to control – although leaving dead seed heads on herbaceous plants and growing shrubs that hold their red berries through the winter are sometimes recommended.

But gardeners could go so much further: if winter snow is reliable in a district, plantings and hard landscape features can be planned to enhance the magical silence. Frost protectors, for instance, can be dull, but they do not need to be. We have taken many aspects of Japanese gardening, but not to our knowledge their exquisite structures designed to protect plants through the winter: *yuki-tsuri* (snow suspenders) and *wara-maki* (straw binding) may have the same intention as a mulch of old bracken, but their effect is magical and part of the magic is knowing how much effort went into their intricate creation. Even the split cane domes that Andrew Crace makes to protect against frost look exquisite with a light covering of snow.

Sliding a solid object out on to a frozen stretch of water gives a similar feeling: a bench, or a pot with something growing in it – a small piece of topiary or a well-bespangled small Christmas tree would be wonderful – or even a wicker basket hill of fruit. They force a sensation that things are not quite what they seem; that this water is now a weight-bearing solid material instead of a fluid weight-absorbing one; that the frost queen or the northern wind has cast a magic spell over the winter garden.

Americans are more open than Britons to extending Christmas decorations to the garden: one of the delights of New England in December is the enormous variety of lighting effects on display. In an otherwise natural woodland, a single tree ablaze with white fairy lights can make a whole Christmas experience out of a garden.

Below
This twisted wooden sculpture has been positioned to look like a huge serpent that is winding its way through Grizedale Forest.

Nor are temporary effects necessarily dependent on cold weather. We decorate our houses for celebrations without a qualm, well aware that these often extravagant garnishes will have to be moved quite soon before they become tawdry, overblown and messy. But if we bring flowers and greenery (including Christmas trees) into the house for decoration, why are we so slow to take household decorations outside? A small orchard with a huge red ribbon bow around each tree, or a strip of tin-foil catching light and reflection; helium balloons in bunches 'growing' in an otherwise conventional herbaceous border; Christmas tree lights and other decorations on deciduous trees – perhaps an apple tree decorated through the winter with red glass baubles – there is an infinite range of decoration that

could be utilized in gardens to delight and entrance visitors, if we weren't so terrified of showing-off, or being 'vulgar'.

Some temporary garden features require more thought and preparation, but fireworks are a traditional way of making outdoor magic. Some gardeners are using modern technology to get mysterious and fairy effects. The smoke machine would seem to have a great deal of potential; fog and mist are deeply ingrained through pantomime and film as part of our experience of the eerie and ghostly. Bunny Guinness showed a garden at Chelsea in 1998; alongside a flight of stone steps lay stone dragons, and from their long snouts at the foot of the steps 'smoke' (in reality ultra-fine water-spray) puffed delicately. In both Japan and Sweden smoke has been used in gardens to create mists and fogs, lying in hollows or swirling across vistas.

And finally two artists who have worked in deliberately temporary media. In his book *Wood*, the artist Andy Goldsworthy presents a series of pictures of the same tree – a huge hardwood with one long outreaching branch. Goldsworthy decorated this branch over and over again, in ever-changing ways using all sorts of different materials, some of them very quick to decay (he reported that with the line of dandelion heads it was a race against time to create the golden line before the flowers started to fade). In a very important sense Goldsworthy was not gardening in this exercise; he was creating a series of arrangements to be photographed – the 'art' was the photograph rather than the objects being photographed, but the distinction is a very narrow one, as is demonstrated by the fact that *The Garden* ran an article on the book. Certainly this title – and his previous one, *Stone*, which presented a rather similar series of arrangements of natural rocks – are worth investigating for ideas of how temporary garden features can create moods and moments of strange magic.

Lawnmowing can make a wonderful transient garden feature, lasting a few days or longer, depending on what is executed; but the contrasting stripes or patterns mown into a lawn are a medium-term decoration compared to the magic of Chris Parsons' dew-brushing patterns. In the early 1990s, Chris Parsons worked as a groundsman in Buckinghamshire and among his duties was the maintenance of some bowling greens. To keep the delicate grass free of fungal infestations bowling greens have to be kept free of dew, particularly in the cool of autumn.

In the autumn of 1990, Chris Parsons realized, almost by accident, that the wide dew brushes could be used to make patterns in the lawn, dark and light areas emerging as the brush was dragged one way or the other across the almost perfectly smooth surface. This is no easy art form: errors are irremediable, and the conditions required for the work cannot be relied on – he needed a cold, but frost-free, windless night followed by a sunny, still morning. For these reasons dew patterns work best in October. He had about 2 hours to make the patterns, which when they pleased him he photographed from about 12 metres (40 feet) up a near-by tree (all the photographs of Chris Parson's work are taken from the same angle across the bowling green because of the need to be high above it, facing the morning sun). By midday the effect will have vanished.

'The appeal of this art form to me,' Chris Parsons has said, 'lies in its transient quality. Apart from one pattern, which was seen by a group of young footballers, all the other patterns were seen only by me and by my colleagues and once by a visiting friend.'

This is art and gardening and a game that Chris Parsons is playing with extremely basic and simple equipment. Gardens do not have to be permanent to be magical; there is a special magic in a willingness to let go, to let the creative moment be just for itself, a spell woven by a master magician pulling together a cold, clear, windless night and a bright, still, autumn morning. It is in the exploitation of these natural changes that magic gardens are made.

Opposite

Outdoor Christmas lights are much more common in the USA than in Europe. Most of them are based on traditional designs, but occasionally something as simple as this fiery arch in a pine forest in northwest Connecticut will stop you in your tracks.

Passions of the Mind

6

*I found the situation of that place much convenient
for the trial of my philosophical conclusions.*

FRANCIS BACON (1561–1626)

WHEN FRANCIS BACON WROTE this description of his garden at Twickenham, he was bestowing on the garden the highest praise he could think of. A garden was *meant* to be a place where the owner could explore his philosophical, or in more modern language his intellectual, ideas most fully. The garden would support this endeavour not just by being a peaceful spot to study such matters, but also by expressing the ideas in its situation – that is its place in the world, its landscape, in its design or layout, in its ornamentation (which included its horticultural effects), and in its function. The overall effects and the smaller details of gardens should both reflect the gardeners' personal belief systems and remind, exhort, encourage and inspire them to live up to their ideals.

For example, if you are a person with a great love of solitude, but think morally you ought to spend more time with your family, your garden should contain not only a secret place – with perhaps a single seat at the end of a path too narrow for more than one person to walk along – but also a dining area, or some artefact that requires more than one person to fulfil its purpose, such as a see-saw or a chess board. Or, to take an idea that would have been entirely alien to Francis Bacon, if you believe that your children need free and creative space to develop their imaginations and practise their creativity, it is no use designing a garden in which they will have to be confined to and only allowed to play in a fenced off corner with a tidy sandpit. Instead, you will either have to think very creatively about how to manage your water features so that the toddlers do not drown, or go without water features altogether.

These are domestic examples. The challenge comes when the 'philosophical conclusions' that you wish to put on 'trial' are more abstract, more profound and more general. It is extremely difficult for us to break away from the idea that a garden is a 'natural' place. Yet as soon as we start to think about it, it is obviously a ridiculous notion. More often we are really describing a sort of sentimental and lazy nostalgia for a golden age that never existed and that we would not have liked if it had: an age without lawnmowers, plant nurseries, disease-resistant hybrids and most of the flowering plants that we think of as 'traditional', and with a grim necessity to get in enough vegetables for the long, cold winter, or to starve.

Opposite
*Johnny Woodford and
Cleve West combine their
talents as artist and
garden designer to create
spaces that are often
symbolic or emblematic,
or that explore specific
themes. Here we see Cleve
West's own garden, with
its creative use of shape
and perspective.*

Luckily there are, and always have been, gardeners who are not fashion victims, and who, for whatever reasons, have the intellectual curiosity, the commitment of time and energy, and an adequate (which usually means excellent) understanding of horticultural skills or of construction techniques or of both. We are going to begin this chapter by looking in some detail at a few such gardens – those which seem to us to reflect Bacon's ideal but within a contemporary aesthetic, and with 21st-century intellectual concerns.

There are no doubt many individuals who have pushed this concept into new gardening forms whom we have either failed to identify or who do not want their work publicised; but there are four great contemporary gardens, all of them quite well known, that seem to us to demonstrate how a strong philosophical concept is being expressed. Little Sparta, in Lanarkshire, Scotland, is the garden of the artist and poet Ian Hamilton Finlay. It is, in a formal and concrete sense, a 'sacred grove'. In it he is trying to express a classical understanding of harmony, and a deep concern about secularization – a loss of a sense of the sacred in art and in society. Ivan Hicks' Garden in Mind in West Sussex is far more playful, and takes as its points of departure two apparently incompatible philosophic ideas: Celtic numerology and surrealism! Prospect Cottage, near Lydd in Kent, the coastal home and garden of the late film director and artist Derek Jarman, challenges currently held notions of nature and art – and their relationship to life and death. And back in southern Scotland, Charles Jencks' Garden of Cosmic Speculation explores ways of expressing in landscape and gardening terms the radical ways that post-Einsteinian physics and mathematics have changed our perception of the world.

In a sense none of these gardens fit very happily into gardening books. Certainly nothing we had read about them prepared us for the experience of seeing them, and having written about and photographed them we know why. The writers end up describing fragments, ripping out the gardens' hearts and minds as it were, and presenting them as a series of features – not because of ill-will or stupidity, but because there is not an adequate gardening vocabulary to encompass them. This fragmentation is extremely tempting: it would be possible, for example, to break all these gardens up and then insert bits of them into the other chapters of this book. The Garden of Cosmic Speculation has been carved out of the landscape; its foundation, as we mentioned in that chapter, is in the ancient tradition of earthworks, or the more modern idiom of 'Land Art'. The Garden in Mind is immensely witty, full of visual puns and laughter. Little Sparta is a deeply magical place and fulfils all the criteria of those gardens, along with much of their sensibility. And Prospect Cottage sits as contemplatively on its beach as any of the gardens in the chapter on reflection. In a sense it is the great difficulty of transferring these gardens to a different medium (writing, photography) that makes one aware that they are works of art: that is, they are single representations which need to be taken as a whole; the medium and the message are integrated. As with any work of art you cannot describe them and tell the reader 'what they are about'. They simply are.

We have decided to tackle the matter head-on, however, because of our awareness, which has driven this whole book, that there is currently a serious and widespread deficiency: gardeners are often either unaware of what we are calling their 'reference' – their points of departure, their own gardens' historical place – or they are aware of it but have not developed a contemporary idiom to express it. Ian Hamilton Finlay describes himself as 'pure classicist' – and after talking to him we agree; but we have all been taught to see classicism as a style rather than as a philosophy. Ian Hamilton Finlay is expressing the classicist philosophy in a new style. It was not easy to see Little Sparta as a 'classical garden', because it is not an imitation, a reproduction, a copy of a classical garden. It is a modern garden created by a classicist.

For these sorts of reasons, we found looking at and photographing these gardens demanding and tiring. This was our problem – the gardeners themselves could not have been kinder or more helpful in finding the time and the words to describe and explain what they were doing. The struggle that we both

Opposite
Ian Hamilton Finlay's garden in Lanarkshire, Scotland, grows out of the surrounding countryside and stimulates the mind. Here, a quotation from Virgil's Eclogues, *'Folding in the last sheep', transforms an otherwise simple dry stone enclosure into an artwork.*

experienced to *see* what they were up to proves exactly how badly we all need to re-think. We can only hope that our difficulties will not reduce the following pages to dense and unilluminating prose, because we cannot stress too strongly that these gardens are real – they are not horticultural theory, nor are they philosophical theses – they are lovely, exhilarating and beautiful places. The pleasure they give as gardens is their justification. Ivan Hicks reported his amused delight when he heard a small child announce to its mother as they went round the Garden in Mind, 'This can't be a real garden, it's too much fun.'

Little Sparta is perched high on the side of a valley in the Pentland Hills, above the little village of Dunsyre. Here, the Scottish Border hills are wide and curvaceous, though bare; even the valleys are not heavily wooded, and above them is the scrub of heather moors. This is sheep-farming country and a place of wide views. But the sense of timelessness is false; this countryside has been denuded of its original forests, fought over for centuries, and its way of life remains under threat from Edinburgh urbanization, tourism and the decline in agriculture. When Ian Hamilton Finlay came to Little Sparta there was the farmhouse, standing virtually naked on the hillside, surrounded by a few brushy rowan trees and one great pine – hardly enough to soften the harshness. This was not a likely place for a man who 'is in love with groves' and 'likes the idea of harmony – of stone and plants and trees' to start a garden. It is difficult, but important to realize just how much has had to be done to transform the hillside into the garden, because Ian Hamilton Finlay insists that he is not a gardener (by which he means a horticulturist) and because it is essential to grasp that there is nothing 'everlasting' or 'natural' about the garden he has made. The house is still approached by a steep, rough, gated farm track, and gives little advance warning of its extravagant (not in terms of money, but of density of meaning) emblematic garden.

The notion of an emblematic garden would have been entirely comprehensible before the 19th century, and indeed many were made. Most simply, the term means a garden that can be 'read' at two levels

Within a small wood at Little Sparta, this pyramid, like many other related sculptures, is designed to encourage meditation on mortality.

– first it is a garden – not admittedly an ordinary garden, but one that offers many of the satisfactions that gardens offer: walks, views, plants, places to sit and rhythm and changes of mood. But at the same time, each of the individual areas can be read as symbolic, as representing something beyond themselves, such as the state of humanity, or the world, or God. The problem is that in our fissured and secularized culture it is very difficult to decode the symbols, to be sure what they do mean. Ian Hamilton Finlay, despite his insistence that he left school at 14 and did not have a classical education, has a complex sweep of subtle reference; a range of languages and loves that can be hard to follow.

For instance, around the garden are a substantial number of plaques, statues and tablets with a name (often a woman's name) carved on them in beautiful roman script, followed by a couple of letters and numbers. Were these numbers part of a catalogue system, references to a classical text, a dating code? No, they are the port numbers of the ships, whose names are carved with them – the lettering that all sea-going craft must carry. Without that information we found we very easily fell into the posture of the child we described earlier (see page 56) who was able to read a complicated treasure hunt, or route map, out of the quotations that Anne Wareham had attached to her trees in the wood, even though no such trail existed.

Little Sparta is divided into four parts: a domestic garden, a wood, a wilderness and a park. The front garden is shaded and protected from the hills by hedges and trees, and is laid out with a bow to formality. There is a central sunken 'pool', which is dry, and paths that lead you round plantings and statuary. Behind the house, a sunnier area is taken up with a large pond, framed along one side with old farm buildings, one of which has been elaborately ornamented to make it look like a garden temple. Behind the pool is a shaded part, including a funerary walk – with tombs and a pyramid.

One leaves this domestic section by a wicket gate into the wood, or grove. Here, entrancing tiny paths, mown or brick laid, intertwining and maze-like, lead up to the top of the garden, while a channel of water leads back down as a series of pools, falls and a stream, which the paths cross – by bridges or stepping stones. The planting is naturalistic, native trees shade the paths and the water, and might even be called romantic were the whole area not lavishly ornamented with statuary. These dappled shady paths and their thought-provoking artefacts create not simply the mood but the activity of Bushell's 'contemplative groves' – they invite one to share Ian Hamilton Finlay's 'trial of [his] philosophical conclusions.'

Running along the hill, parallel to the grove, is a little wilderness, in the Baconian tradition – that is to say a highly disciplined and designed reflection of the wild. The 'wild' here are the undulating heather moors, and the long views down the valley or across the hills. To 'match' the valley and river below there is a river here, made artificially by damming and management, and this presents the walker with a view of lakes – or rather, since the respect for the local environment is so strong, of small, wild, golden lochs.

And below the 'moor', back alongside the house, Ian Hamilton Finlay has recently laid out a miniature English park in the style of Charles Bridgeman, with mown grass, paths, more formal groves, vistas, statuary and an undulating landscape. Thence one can return either past beehives set in a row among cherry trees and a small vegetable plot, to the demesne, or through a formal gateway to the wood.

Nothing in this sounds particularly challenging. Lovely, interesting, well thought through, but hardly radical. But nothing is quite as it seems. Take the formal archway that leads from the grove into the park – red brick and rectilinear, it is surmounted in the 18th-century style with what at first sight look like reproduction traditional pineapples, but are in fact model hand grenades. Similarly, a charming corner of the front garden, a little circle of dark pine trees underplanted with hosta, is ornamented with a group of white stone carvings of aircraft-carriers (they double as bird tables in winter), and the cheerfully coloured stakes that support the vegetables or hold back overflowing perennials from the pathways are painted in camouflage patterns.

Ian Hamilton Finlay was born at sea, loves ships and recognizes in the Lanarkshire hills the shapes and rhythms of the ocean waves; in his garden he is much engaged with the creation and representation of 'maritime mythology.' There are ships everywhere – including the port numbers mentioned above, and the sinister shape of a black submarine conning tower that rises over the moorland loch – but there are even more references to waves. The 'earthworks' of his park mirror the hills around them, and emphasize their wavelike structure – the hills look more like waves after you have seen the park than they did before. Such larger effects are replicated on a smaller scale – beside the stepping stones across one of the pools in the woodland is a plaque that gives the dictionary definition of the word 'ripple' (n. a wind, a fluting of a liquid element).

Classical references also abound. The silhouette of Daphne is pursued through the woodland by Apollo – cut out of sheet metal and painted red and green – a reference perhaps not only to transformation and classical mythology, but also to Andrew Marvell's 17th-century poem *The Garden* – a philosophical meditation on gardens and the imagination: 'Apollo haunted Daphne so/Only that she might laurel grow'.

Even more direct are the references to Virgil, and specifically to the *Georgics* and the *Eclogues* in which the poet/philosopher laid out his dream of the rural life for the philosophical soul. The sheepfold (with its quotation from the *Eclogues*), the beehives, the tidy vegetables and the winding pathways, are drawn from this source, as are many of the quotations. At the highest point of the garden a spring lets the water in from the hills; and carved upon the fountain is the Virgilian quote *Hic gelida fontes, Hic mollia prata* (Here are cool springs, here soft meadows).

This quotation brings us to a central feature of this garden: the number of words – usually beautifully and formally carved into stone – that it contains. Ian Hamilton Finlay believes in words – he is himself a reputed concrete poet and artist. Linking words, poetry, articulation and reference with the natural is the heart of the project, its 'religion.' as it were. The garden, like the rest of Ian Hamilton Finlay's work, is a protest, or rather a standard set up, against the secularization and urbanization of contemporary culture.

Lest all this seems very earnest, it is important to add that Ian Hamilton Finlay is at one level extremely witty – the garden is packed with visual 'jokes'. A milestone on one long winding path announces 'The Wayfarer's Tree. 2yds.' and 1.8 metres (2 yards) away he has planted a *Viburnum lantana*, whose common name is 'the Wayfarer's tree'. In the park is Huff Street – a long avenue closed at the far end, which when completed will contain a series of small seats – somewhere to go when you are in a sulk, or huff. Some of the jokes are more arcane: the aircraft-carrier garden described above is called Homage to the Villa d'Este, because the Renaissance makers of those Italian gardens thought they were replicating Roman paintings; in fact the favourite theme of Roman painting turns out to have been scenes of sea battles – a subject matter ignored in the 16th century, but now reproduced on a Scottish hillside. A small island on the pool near the house is a precise copy of Dürer's famous drawing *The Great Piece of Turf*. It even contains a tablet with Dürer's signature initials carved on it.

But this lightness of touch does not overwhelm the importance of Ian Hamilton Finlay's engagement with contemporary culture. This war has even had a political front. The local council decided that the Garden Temple was a selling gallery and should be charged the commercial rates. They simply refused to accept that a garden temple was a possible function for a building – it was not on their computer and that was that. For 15 years Ian Hamilton Finlay contested this, and tried to use the situation as a way of attracting interest to the nature and history of art. He never paid the tax demand, but cannot see his fight as a victory – rather as a cause for deep mourning.

Like David Rosewarne as a 'priest' in his magical garden church, however differently expressed, Ian Hamilton Finlay does see the garden (his own and as a cultural form) as a deeply spiritual entity – a point of mediation between culture and nature. He says he cannot see the whole garden as a work of art, although he would like to, because it has taken so many years to make and cannot therefore have the singleness of vision and unity that a work of art requires. None the less, this is a garden *about* art and society, a passionate and personal expression of the state of culture, and a mourning for a world from which the lesser gods of field and grove have been banished. Here they will find sanctuary, his garden proclaims. One of the plaques sums this up.

> All the noble sentiments of my heart, all its most praiseworthy
> impulses – I could give free rein in the midst of this solitary wood.

By contrast, Ivan Hicks' Garden in Mind is an optimistic, cheerful, riotous place. But it is also about the meeting point of nature and culture, about what gardens are meant to be, what they are *for*. Like Little Sparta, it is creedal: it is the way it is because its maker is who he is – and he has allowed his convictions to drive the design and execution of his extraordinary garden. The difficulty here is that the convictions, the points of reference themselves, are extremely complex: you could sum up the garden, perhaps, by saying it is a speculation on what might happen if Salvador Dalí met the White Goddess.

Ivan Hicks is a tree person, a tree artist – trees are the medium of his artistic expression. As trees have a tendency to want to sculpt themselves, a tree artist has a problem. If the same artist also venerates trees, recognizing that life on this planet is largely dependent on them for its vital supplies of oxygen, then it might be but a short step to a sentimental version of a 'green' Celtic philosophy. Luckily, Ivan Hicks coupled these commitments with a strong sense of the surreal and a direct involvement in surrealist thought.

Ivan Hicks first studied Wood Sciences at the London School of Furniture, but quickly realized that he was more interested in living trees than in dead ones. So instead he went to Merrist Wood College to learn arboriculture. Once qualified he took a job looking after an arboretum at West Dean – the garden

Right

In the Garden in Mind, Ivan Hicks uses his knowledge of plants in an extraordinary way. He sculpts and manipulates them, often combining other materials, to create a work of surreal art. This practice invites the viewer to explore further, both in the garden itself and into what we believe gardens 'should be'.

of Edward James, the great patron of the surrealist movement. In what was clearly a strong collegiality, Ivan Hicks travelled with James to Mexico, Italy and Ireland to create features for his gardens there, and this gave him an opportunity to compare tree culture – in both senses of the word, grown and thought about – in different contexts.

After James' death, Ivan Hicks decided that he wanted to create his own garden, and started looking about for a site. In 1991, the BBC was making a series of programmes about dream gardens. The programme makers came to West Dean to discover that Ivan Hicks was leaving, so they gave him £500 to create a 'surrealist' garden from scratch. Hicks leased the Lower Walled Garden at Stansted Park in Hampshire and set to work with considerable haste. The origins of Garden in Mind were thus part commission and part desire, but over the last eight years the garden has settled down and developed.

It is easier to see Garden in Mind as a work of art because it is tidily framed by old red brick walls; it is contained in precisely the way that a picture is. Frames allow a freedom within them, a liberated space for the imagination, and when one first enters the garden it is this sense of an imagination set free that strikes home.

Two factors impinge immediately. There are a great number of things in the garden that are not normally found there: old iron ware, household furniture, rusty metal and shop window mannequins. There is also a huge 'balloon' – a ship's bumper-buoy – painted very blue with little white clouds (copying Magritte's trademark background) and suspended within a pergola – a chunk of sky brought down to the ground. And the trees are not behaving as they 'should'. Some have two or even three trunks, but only one head. Others grow in the shape of Gothic cathedrals, or they divide in the middle to form perfect circles. There is a young living oak bridge (the plan is that it will be strong enough for one of Ivan Hicks' children to walk across to celebrate the millennium) that spans a rock stream, which flows into a water pond. There is a 'relaxing centre': a 1.5-metre (5-foot) wide circle, planted with six aspens (*Populus tremuloides*), which have been plashed and trimmed, their sideways-growing branches woven into each other while those that would have grown into the middle of the circle, or directly away from it, have been cut off. Now there is a sort of hollow tube inside the circle, and a seat has been placed there for quiet reflection amid the quivering dancing leaves.

There is a ginkgo tunnel, which – when it is matured and trained by pulling the tops together and tying them so that they will graft into one and then rigorously rubbing off the interior shoots – will, we were assured, take on an architectural form like that of a high Gothic church.

The despised leylandii has had its fast-growing quality rigorously trained: 12 of them form a tight circle, trimmed into a tower on the outside, but inside clipped and tied together to form a cylinder, each tree stabilizing its neighbours. At the ground level there is a door into the centre, and then a ladder that allows you to climb about 2.5 metres (8 feet) up to a viewing platform with a window frame. It is a treehouse, not just a house in a tree. Beside the tower, incidentally, there is a raised vegetable bed. This is the tower from the fairy story of Rapunzel, who was doomed to imprisonment because her pregnant mother could not resist the brassicas in her wicked neighbour's garden.

This extravagant profusion of the unexpected disguises the fact that the garden is laid out on the most formal principles. There are three long axes which run the whole length of the garden – very much on the pattern of a medieval cathedral. Two narrower side aisles, each with very different atmospheres, run the whole way to the furthest wall, offering vistas through peculiar tunnels and archways. The central axis is more open. It runs from a ruined archway and gate, over a basin, across a 'topiary' sun (golden lonicera cut into curved horns or rays) to a central mound, and beyond to a bridge, a summerhouse and a pool. The mound sits in the centre of a grass circle, and off to the sides of the main *allée* are a series of small

Opposite

Using whatever materials come to hand, Ivan Hicks creates 'cartoons' within the whole work that is Garden in Mind. Here, objects and plants are combined to create an intricate landscape in one tiny corner of the garden.

gardens. Since this whole fantasy world covers only 0.2 hectare (½ an acre), small does mean small, but they are quite distinct gardens framed in their own plantings. There is a lateral axis that runs across the centre of the mound, which from this point of view becomes the High Altar of the Gothic cathedral. Beyond it, the bridge and pool could also be seen as the Lady Chapel, particularly as the final focus of the main axis is a group of three blue women – mannequin dummies painted once again with Magritte clouds.

Once the brain has calmed down from the overload of the objects, it becomes clear that the garden is not restless at all, but serene on its carefully calculated and structured ground plan. The proportions are those of the ancient Celtic number systems, focused around the number seven, and of movements forward and back that inform the layout of true Celtic labyrinths. The mound is made from the spoil of the basin; they balance in size as they symbolically acknowledge the womb and the navel; the masculine and the feminine; the cosmic principles of wholeness. This movement between the most ancient of forms and the most outrageous and bizarre outer reaches of the human imagination (conscious or unconscious as in dreams) is the underlying framework of all serious surrealist art, as well as of the many traditional gardening theories. However childlike much of this garden may seem, it is the product of a rigorous and adult brain.

This is why, having laid such careful schemes on his landscape, Ivan Hicks can be entirely casual about whether or not people take up his references. This is a garden and, like a surrealist painting, the exact meanings and implications do not need to be decoded all the time. For example, there is another structure, besides the formal one, to this garden – it can be read as the inevitable journey from youth to age. The three axes of the garden are different routes to the same end. As you enter the garden you look straight down one of the narrower side axes – 'the straight and narrow' Ivan Hicks calls it. It is simple and planted with bright light colours. The sky balloon, all summery and bright, and a reflecting ball hang there. Some people's lives are like that, and some are serpentine, complex, various or even dark, as the snake path beside this straight path implies, but all paths arrive at the dark end of the garden eventually. It really does not matter if you 'get it' or not; you can wander through or around the garden in any order you like, the more you are amused and diverted *en route* the happier Ivan Hicks will be, because in the end the structure and meaning are there, engaging him and sometimes, in whole or in part, engaging the visitor as well. Meanwhile, they provide an underlying frame for his individual choices, just as the wall itself frames the whole garden.

The Garden in Mind asks some telling questions. One of the most obvious ones is about what is natural and what is not. In the centre of his mound Ivan Hicks has planted an 'ironic tree', with dangling glass prisms instead of leaves. It is 'ironic' because it is made of iron, because it is 'unnatural' in a place that celebrates natural trees and because it is planted as a tree of peace in a world in which there is no peace; an emblem of 'nature's principles corrupted'. A short distance from it are two paulownia trees – 'real' trees, though by no means 'natural' to southern England. These trees are energetically controlled, pruned right back to a single bud for each branch. Any side shoots are rubbed out diligently, and this makes the remaining leaves grow 'unnaturally' large, in tufts at the end of the branches. It also makes the trunk grow in steps, right-angled turns that, given their smooth grey form, look metallic and every bit as artificial as the iron tree. They also look very much like the trees drawn by small children, and Ivan Hicks commented on how much children like them. They force one to question the whole division between natural and unnatural, real and fake.

This theme is repeated around the mound's circle: tall iron abstract statues, made out of the detritus of the Second World War's coastal fortifications, stand ominously as sentinels to the magic mound, or as reminders of how human wars have damaged the world, or simply as wonderful shapes against the Hampshire sky. They have exactly the same shape in silhouette, however, as a mammoth yucca's dead flower heads from last year, which had not been removed when we were there in April. The antique and rusted garden roller beside them can roll nothing because it has metal spikes attached to it; it is a surreal roller. Elsewhere, in a homage to Magritte, there is a garden called The Future of the Office, where living sempervivums creep through an old typewriter. A section of one of the paths of the side axis is made of sharp gravel and planted with prickly *Argemone*. The comfortable way to cross this 'natural' area is on smooth round harrow blades, now laid flat but originally designed to cut the land up. The wooden posts of a 'dead' banister are suspended from strings so that they move in the breeze; mirrors throw back reflections, or reveal plants otherwise hidden from the path; teasels are encouraged to grow on the paths because they collect tiny lakes in their leaves, which sparkle like mirrors.

Ivan Hicks, like most people with truly original gardens, insists that he is doing nothing new: there has been a long tradition throughout Europe of manipulating living plants in arbours, bowers and archways. None the less, this is not extended topiary because the growing form of the plant strongly influences the use he puts it to. While pure traditional topiary tried to dominate the plant entirely, he chooses paulownia or leylandii or aspen precisely because of its inherent growing tendencies, which he can then 'play with' as though he were giving the tree the shape of its own dreams.

Ivan Hicks can make his garden work not just because he is a creative artist, singularly undominated by garden fashions, with a strong sense of wit – and not just because he is self-aware and reflective about his own points of reference – but also because he has an immense knowledge of plants, especially trees. The Garden in Mind may not look like a 'plantsman's garden', in the sense that it has no horticultural stamp collection feel to it, but it is the garden of an arboriculturist. For all its apparent informality and sense of casualness, the plants in this garden are not left to their own devices for a single minute; they are managed by the gardener – given new forms and new voices out of the dreams and ideas of their maker. This is another way in which this garden can be seen as true art: the artist has a real mastery of his medium, which provides a freedom to express what he wants to with it.

In his final years Derek Jarman himself wrote a lot about Prospect Cottage, the garden that became his final meditation on transience. Since his death it has been further photographed and written about by others, so much so that it does not seem appropriate here to do more than mention it, as a garden created in an improbable context to express the awareness of approaching death and the great rhythm of life set in counterpoint to the individual's decline and disappearance. Derek Jarman's garden consists of the few plants that can be persuaded to grow in the inhospitable and virtually soil-less rocky beach, under the shadow of the Dungeness nuclear power station. We have already described it as a garden created out of its own landscape and here it is worth recommending Jarman's own book, *Modern Nature*, which he wrote in parallel with the making of the garden and which – in remarkably accessible language – describes how the individual pieces of flotsam, jetsam and beach debris were used together with the planting. Although almost all the materials of the garden were 'found' by what can best be called careful accident, they were none the less worked into the garden with the greatest care to express his philosophy in much the same way as he had used images in his films.

Opposite

Prospect Cottage, near Lydd in Kent, is a unique example of how native plants can be blended with the flotsam and jetsam thrown up on the beach to create a lasting image.

Charles Jencks is currently writing a book about his garden near Dumfries, Scotland, which he started with Maggie Keswick. The Garden of Cosmic Speculation forms part of a 12-hectare (30-acre) garden and consists of earthworks, lakes and constructions on a very large scale. Jencks' points of departure are numerous. Maggie Keswick wrote an influential book on the Chinese philosophy of gardening, and when the two of them dug out some bathing lakes in the 1980s she wanted to use the spoil to create a curved rampart to represent a land dragon. As the planning and work went forward, Charles Jencks added the idea that the shapes of the 122-metre (400-foot) earthwork should also represent the theory of folding – a complex explanation of how strings of amino acids form three-dimensional structures. The couple also constructed a 20-metre (65-foot) mount with double spiral paths, which was both a symbol of the pathway to heaven and a model of the DNA double helix. This set of structures has a dramatic quality, generated out of its basic purity of line – water and mown grass and huge scale. Other features are smaller, more elaborate and often more playful, but everything in the garden is designed with some reference to scientific discoveries – from the 10 garden gates made of metal strips twisted to represent solidon waves, to the Black Hole Terrace constructed of aluminium and turf that demonstrates the repetition across scale of fractal geometry and the singularity which physicists now believe was the point of creation. The old vegetable garden has been renamed the Physics Garden (a pun on the physick or medicinal garden of old) and, still under construction, contains a wide range of features representing various aspects of the human senses, while at the same time playing with new forms of old features, such as a startling grotto – an emblem of sight.

Left

In the Garden of Cosmic Speculation, near Dumfries, Charles Jencks explores how the landscape can be used to express ideas of a complex scientific nature. The massive earthworks shown here represent the theory of folding.

Right
*John and Anne Bracey
have constructed some
remarkable features in
their Devonshire garden,
many of which have been
shaped through the use of
mathematical equations.*

Despite this plethora of intellectual stimuli, Charles Jencks has insisted that 'Beauty is always uppermost in my mind, or at least making things look striking. But you can't cheat – you have to show the theories as they are…. In this garden [we] worked to create a resonance so that everything relates to everything else, so making a symbol as opposed to a sign. The idea of a symbol is to excite you to want to know what is going on.' The garden is meant to make you think. At the same time it is a deliberate and radical critique of contemporary garden design: 'We both got fed up with English garden design and English gardens. How many ideas are there in contemporary landscaping? I think landscape needs new ideas, a new lease of life.'

These four gardens are exceptional in the distance they have managed to take ideas not, at least at present, normally associated with gardening. In each case they have created unique and exciting gardens, which are intellectually stimulating as well as pleasing to be in. But there are other 'ideas' that can be built into gardens, perhaps more simply, which extend the intellectual range and reflect the dearly held passions or convictions of their designers – or alternatively challenge visitors to garden themselves in new, enjoyable and interesting ways.

They are not of course the only gardeners who have used non-garden related intellectual concepts to define the structure of their garden. On a much smaller scale John and Ann Bracey at Scypen in Devon have used very contemporary scientific concepts in both the underlying structural planning of their garden and in some of its specific features. John Bracey is a retired architect who designed and made the garden and house, which he converted from an old cowshed. Throughout there is an intimate connection between the house and the garden around it, with two terraces built within the outreaching walls of the building itself – walled gardens or open rooms or both. From these enclosures the small, 0.2 hectare (½ acre) garden tips quite sharply downwards and offers a wonderful view of the sea. The price of this view is the sea winds that constantly batter the garden and, to some extent, control the planting and planning.

Within this framework, however, John Bracey has constructed some immensely pleasing and sophisticated structures, all of which take their initial impulse from a scientific or mathematical principle. A remarkably beautiful sinuous dry stone wall with an elegant slate cap takes its shape from the Fibonacci number series.

The Fibonacci series is created when the sum of the previous two numbers in the series determine the next number – 0, 1, 1, 2, 3, 5, 8, 13, 21, 34, etc. Plotted on a graph these form a spiral, which is now believed to be the underlying structure of many natural phenomena, such as snail shells and even the branch and leaf arrangements of many trees. Fibonacci numbers – along with Mandebrot sets (which are suggested in the shapes of a pebble edging to the nearby water feature) – are part of the new mathematical science of fractals and chaos theory that appears in many ways to be the maths of natural structures.

John Bracey readily admits that he does not take this too literally, but the curved wall strongly suggests that the underlying use of so abstruse a science provides a more satisfying shape than a random 'what looks nice' approach would have done; and it is a deeply enjoyable game for him. A second, different, but co-ordinating wall, which winds out to meet this scientific one, is arranged in the shape of a question mark. Bracey claims that it is meant to ask 'why all this gardening?' But for the millennium he is making a stone globe – a round map of the world – to form the full stop at the end of the question mark. It will be mounted so that it can revolve: although not yet in place it is an exquisite piece, perhaps 0.6 metre (2 feet) in diameter and with the land masses marked out in great detail. It implies that the question is not altogether frivolous, although it may well be deeply playful.

In the same spirit he has designed a water feature based on the underlying structures of DNA. The highest point of the structure is his fountain of life – a set of slate roof tiles arranged in a spiral down which water drips into the ponds in a genuinely random, ever-changing pattern. In the chapter on reflection we described John Bracey's bottle glass den, in which the arrangement of the round bottle bottoms is also mathematically determined to create an ever repeating series of prime numbers, although he insists that he observed this accidentally in the course of working on the project. Another of John Bracey's gardening principles is that he recycles rigorously, that it is wrong to spend serious money on a garden. The most expensive thing in the garden, apart from the plants (though even they are mainly gleanings from other people's gardens) is the cement he has used in the construction of these features. Presently he is collecting spoil from other projects to level a part of the garden so that he can have a croquet lawn. In one sense the whole garden has a unity, a connectedness, because each project depends on other projects – a slow and organically integrated development. At its own small scale the garden seems as much informed by intellectual ideas and their place in a search for a wholeness as any of the larger gardens discussed above.

Paul Cooper is a garden designer who uses modernity very differently, but equally decisively. Light and shade and their management have always been important considerations in garden design, and he has taken this forward in a very literal way. In a London garden he has created a light show – projecting contemporary works of art on to a wall at one end of the garden; a new and quickly changeable *trompe-l'oeil* or mural, which in one sense is entirely in the spirit of Pratolino and in another dependant on electricity and related modern technologies. Perhaps more than anyone else we have mentioned in this book Paul Cooper is pushing out the boundaries of what does constitute a garden, and what might constitute one in the next millennium. The OED definition 'a piece of ground devoted to growing flowers fruit or vegetables' is, in the light of some Zen gardens and Paul Cooper's work, clearly no longer satisfactory. Russell Page's 1962 comment that 'garden making … concerns the relationship of the human being to his natural surroundings' begs fundamental questions about what is natural. Is a city a 'natural surrounding'? How will we garden in space? How necessary are concerns such as gravity or atmosphere to a sense of gardening? These sorts of science-and-culture questions, which are being asked seriously in scientific, astronautical circles are being raised in practise in Paul Cooper's designs.

There are two traditional features that have addressed these sorts of questions over several centuries – that bring into the garden scientific or philosophical concepts that have nothing directly to do with

Opposite

Paul Cooper is a designer who refuses to be limited by convention or fashion. In this example, featured at Chelsea in 1999, the drifting planters contrast with the fixed stepping stones – a very new sort of water garden.

horticulture – sundials and mazes. Sundials have nothing intrinsically to do with gardens; in fact they predate gardens. They are scientific instruments with an important social role. From the earliest moments of human history the ability to keep some sort of track of the seasons of the year and the divisions of the day has proved essential. It is widely believed that while Stonehenge was erected between *circa* 2500 and 1500 BC for religious motives, a crucial part of that religion was marking the solstices – in that sense Stonehenge is a massive sundial. The first mention of a recognizable sundial comes from Egypt in about 1300 BC. Before the invention of reliable clocks, sundials had a vital social function and were as likely to be found in public places (churchyards, market squares and university quadrangles) as they were in private homes.

Once clocks had taken over the sundials' social role, however, they moved into more intimate spaces very easily. Gardens have always been understood to have an organic connection with questions about time and its passing, about the relationship between culture and nature, and the sundial is an obvious point of reference. It brings the natural order under the purview of scientific knowledge; while a sundial obviously cannot control the movements of the sun or the planets, it can demonstrate a human ability to understand, reflect and order that movement.

A great deal of knowledge and skill is necessary to construct a sundial, and a sundial that does not properly tell the time cannot give satisfaction. An accurate and beautiful sundial, on the other hand, can please the eye and draw attention to the nature of time – both arbitrary and absolute, both constructed and inevitable – calling into question even basic assumptions such as the standard 24-hour day. This is not the place to unravel the details of sundial construction, but it is proper to draw attention to the fact that garden sundials are as much, or more, about science and philosophy as they are about a sentimental aesthetic of the natural. To place a sundial in a garden is, consciously or not, to make a decisive choice for civilization and science over nature. To the sundial maker the relationship between time and space is always present in the mind, along with the fusion of ideas about mortality and divine illumination. Because a sundial needs to be aligned specifically to its own site, it simultaneously makes a claim both for universality (the sun shines on the just and on the unjust alike) and for locality – stating in the clearest terms the meaning of a garden.

None the less, there is no reason why a sundial should not also be a lovely or a playful thing: Christopher Daniel, chairman of the British Sundial Society and a sundial designer since 1968, has shown in his work the extraordinary range of contemporary design possibilities. At Scypen in Devon, John Bracey, who as we have seen uses scientific ideas to underpin his own extraordinary garden design, has constructed a scientifically correct sundial garden, setting the gnomon in the centre of a circle of thyme as a horticultural joke. At Evergreens near Hull, Philip Brock has made a small sundial that revives a beautiful and almost lost 17th-century tradition of stained-glass sundials while being completely modern in its appearance. David Harber, another professional sundiallist, designs highly contemporary scientific sundials, including some that consciously combine classical themes with contemporary materials – such as his mirrored glass obelisks, which simultaneously cast a shadow and a reflection. But David Harber also uses the science of light and shadow, and the marking of time in other ways: at Chelsea in 1999 he was showing a Millennial Sun Marker

Above

At Evergreens, in Hull, Philip Brock has revived the 17th-century tradition of the stained-glass sundial, showing how scientific ideas can be incorporated into the modern garden.

– two granite monoliths with a single narrow fissure between them, which are to be set up so that the first ray of sunshine of the 21st century will shine directly through them. As such it is a reference to the science of Stonehenge and to our evolving understanding of the movements of the cosmos.

Sundials also, by tradition, have mottoes carved on them, usually making some sort of reference to the passage of time. So strong is this point of connection with words that Ian Hamilton Finlay believes that people who do not feel at ease with words in gardens will absorb them if they are on sundials. This is one reason why he has so many – not necessarily usable ones – at Little Sparta.

Mazes in the form of labyrinths, which we discussed in the chapter on magical gardens (see page 102), have a history as old, and possibly as spiritual, as sundials, but they also came into gardens very early in their intellectual problem-solving form. The first English book devoted to gardening matters, Thomas Hill's *A Most Breife and Pleasant Treatyse* of 1563, mentions both square and round mazes (along with bowling alleys) as desirable garden features, and lays out patterns for both kinds. And in 1598, Joshuah Sylvestre's translation of a French poem, *Eden* by Saluste Du Bartas (1584), has Adam before the fall wandering in a maze:

> Musing, anon through crooked walks he wanders,
> Round-winding rings and intricate meanders
> False guiding paths, doubtfull beguiling strays,
> And right-wrong errors of an endless Maze.

A maze, as opposed to a labyrinth, is conceived as an intellectual challenge. It can take various forms, from the complexity of a high-hedge maze – such as the famous one at Hampton Court near London – to 'clue' mazes, like the one laid out as a pavement that Mr and Mrs Siggers have constructed in their garden near Aylesbury, where solving the maze gives a visitor entry to the rest of the garden.

Below

Mazes and labyrinths have long been used to bring intelligence to a garden. Admittedly, it would be difficult to lose yourself physically in this Californian example, but slowly trace the contours of the labyrinth and you will soon be lost in thought.

Left
In his Cambridgeshire garden, Richard Fort has created a scaled down landscape of rocks and plants. Through this crafted world runs a miniature steam railway.

Maureen and Louis Hankin of Plumsteadville in Pennsylvania wanted a maze, but did not like the feeling of enclosure that yew or beech hedges gave them. So they laid out a 13-metre-square (144-foot-square) maze in cannas; 100,000 orange red cannas, growing up to 2.4 metres (8 feet) tall. All the rhizomes have to be lifted for winter and replanted by hand in the spring, but the sensation of being lost in such a maze of glory sustains their labours.

Although strictly a labyrinth, Andrew Sankey's 5-metre (17-foot) turf maze at Stixwold in Lincolnshire deserves a mention here, because it was laid out for entirely 'intellectual' reasons. He gardens substantially through seed propagation, and needed somewhere to grow on his seedlings, which would protect them from trampling by children, allow the adult gardeners easy access and form an interesting feature in itself. The maze works ideally to all those ends – the turf makes a delightful playground while the earth between provides ideal space for the young plants, which can be reached easily and individually by the gardener.

The carving of mazes into fields of maize takes the feature out of the garden, but just as a sundial planted with thyme makes a pleasing joke so does this fashion, now repeated on several farms across England. Denis and Marion Beare's annual maze has become a major tourist attraction and has grown so complicated that tea-stalls have to be set up to assist mazers on their way. In Kent, Mike and Sue Blee's maize maze is simpler, more truly a labyrinth, but laid out in the shape of a human body, so that you enter at the toes and wander, like a vein, through the inside of the whole person – a Green Man image laid out with agricultural technology.

Aerial photography can give a new satisfaction to the makers of mazes – they can see the overall effect of what they have made in a way that is new. At Reignac sur Inde, Isabelle de Beaufort has created a truly extraordinary maze laid out as the planetary system, with sweeping long arcs representing the orbits and intense complex pathways delineating specific planetary features. Here, science is once again called into play, but – despite the patience of the lost makers of the Nazca lines, who can never have seen the effect of their labours – it seems unlikely that a design so elegant and complex would have been laid out unless there was some opportunity of seeing the whole overall effect.

A truly modern garden, in that it has been designed so that much of its effect depends on flight, has been made by Bernard Holmes at Bernards Farm in Essex. Not only is the garden partially planned for an overhead viewpoint, but an airstrip has been incorporated into the large and complex garden for the convenience of qualified aeronautical garden visitors.

Intellectual ideas other than scientific ones can be channelled into garden designs. At Plant World, a garden and nursery in Newton Abbot in Devon, the owners have laid out 0.8 hectare (2 acres) as a map of the world. Grass lawns and paths represent the oceans, and the land masses are shaped in flowerbeds and planted with botanical subjects originating in the relevant countries. The idea is not to create typical gardens, a Japanese Garden or a Prairie Garden for instance, but to plant quite traditionally using species native to that particular part of the world.

In Dorset, Liz Draper's garden has two miniature villages. She and her husband started creating the villages out of a fascination with miniature plants (not *bonsai* but naturally occurring miniature species, such as a lilac tree that was mature and flowering freely at about 30 cm (12 inches), a beautiful elm tree less than 60 cm (2 feet) tall, minute cotoneasters and azaleas, and a tiny-leaved ivy climbing the walls of an old ruin). However the villages, and especially the larger one (on a 1:25 scale), have somehow taken over. Castle Draper now has a history, and each house has named inhabitants. The village has become a family game, not only in gardening and construction terms but also in the complex jokes and appalling puns that can be found therein. It is hard to describe Castle Draper, but it is an exquisite construction that bubbles over with joy and creativity – with the simple fun that not enough people seem to get from their gardens.

In much the same way, Richard Fort runs a model railway in his garden. The planting and design of the railway section – in an otherwise ordinary garden – is subservient to the railway's needs. The track, with its stations, landscapes the area; the trains, which run on real steam fuelled by tiny butane canisters, are remote controlled; and Richard Fort is looking forward to remote control switching for the points eventually (this is not a cheap form of entertainment). His enthusiasm and pleasure in this aspect of his garden are infectious, and no misplaced gardening pomposity comes between him and his eagerness to share his successes.

In Charlbury in Oxfordshire there is a shop that specializes in selling equipment – from the trains themselves to scaled environments for the trains – for garden railway enthusiasts, so Richard Fort is by no means isolated in his hobby. In Kent, there is a garden with a ridable-sized railway on it; other furnishings take up the theme – a level crossing barrier, for example, forms the front gateway.

For some reason we have decided culturally that tennis, croquet and swimming are respectable gardening activities, which garden designers willingly advise on, elaborate and beautify, whereas other activities such as running railways are not part of a 'proper' garden. Why not? Certainly there must be many more such gardens, and others dedicated to themes and enthusiasms that we have not even thought of. These seem entirely proper garden pursuits – and more people should liberate themselves and enjoy their personal passions, obsessions and delights in their gardens – it is what gardens are and ought to be for.

One slightly more recognized garden 'function' is art. We briefly mentioned art in gardens in the previous chapter (see pages 111–12), but there we were talking about individual pieces of art used as features in a garden. At Broomhill, near Barnstable in Devon, the garden is a selling gallery for contemporary artists. Rinus and Aniet Van de Sande, who run the garden gallery, an indoor gallery and an Art Hotel all on the same site, see the garden primarily as the background for the artworks, rather than the reverse. Because of a real sensitivity both to the artworks and to the environment in which they were being placed, each seems to enhance the other. A good garden gallery, Broomhill made clear, has to set up a relationship between the two – you can no more plonk down quite difficult artworks in a garden as though it were neutral space than you can plonk down plants and think that will give you a garden. Obviously there is a built-in difficulty because the art – one hopes commercially – will not remain there too long and consequently the garden cannot be designed as a single work incorporating the sculptures in the way that gardens need to be able to do, but even within these restrictions Broomhill (and the Hannah Peschar Garden Gallery in Sussex, which is a similar project) are true gardens of ideas, presenting and exploring the old questions about how nature relates to culture, and how that relationship can be expressed.

These sorts of ideas about garden space are developed more fully by the team effort of Johnny Woodford (an artist) and Cleve West (a garden designer). Together they are creating gardens that are very often symbolic or emblematic and explore quite specific themes. These subjects have included ideas about community and play in the bowling alley garden they constructed in Hampshire, or water conservancy in their Hampton Court Show Garden in 1998 and in the new Wetlands Park in Barnes. Cleve West does not commission Johnny Woodford to make art objects to decorate his garden designs, nor does he design gardens to display Johnny Woodford's art – both conceptually and in execution they work together. In many ways their gardens are among the most creative around: strong in colour and in the coherence of concept, while still being clearly and obviously gardens. They tend to work from an 'aesthetic' point of reference – asking Is this lovely? rather than What is this? or How do we inhabit this? They have a boldness of vision, seen partly in their strong use of colour and non-natural materials, partly in the fantasy elements they integrate, and partly in their use of plants *as* ornament. Art is not there to support plants, nor the plants to enhance the sculptural elements – both are there to make a garden a whole and satisfying work in and of itself.

Left

At Broomhill in Devon,
Rinus and Aniet Van de
Sande have successfully
addressed the difficulty
of placing art in the
landscape. Here, Giles
Kent's carved sculpture
sympathetically reflects
and enhances the living
trees around it.

Practical Advice

7

THIS BOOK IS NOT, and was never meant to be, a 'how-to' manual. However, we hope that it may have encouraged and inspired you, and if so you may want some hints on how to move your ideas forward. This section is meant to suggest ways of doing so – it should not be treated as a manual or instruction kit, but as a resource.

A lot of the gardeners in this book have made the features in their gardens themselves; or got someone else to execute their plans for them. This means that each garden has a unique and personal touch that is impossible to reproduce. Many of the techniques used in this book are surprisingly simple, well within the reach of a competent DIY-er or even of a chronic bodger. Some, however, really do need the skills of a professional. If you have any doubts at all in your mind – consult an expert. This includes both planning permission issues – which of course vary from country to country and even, in the UK, from region to region – and technical questions.

Horticultural skills are extensively covered by a wide range of gardening books easily available from bookshops or your local library. We have therefore not made much reference to them. Other projects are also covered by books, but not necessarily gardening books: a survey of the DIY and craft sections of the public library may, directly or indirectly, prove surprisingly helpful. There are good manuals available on an extraordinary range of subjects, from sculpture through carpentry and metalwork to enamel and mosaic work. The basic techniques of decorative painting and the 'faking' of various types of surface, for example, are covered in several interior decor books and magazines. Many modern paints can be successfully applied to exterior surfaces, although they may not react well to temperature extremes and fluctuations, wind and subsidence.

There are also a great many evening classes and residential courses covering specialist topics. Many of the gardeners we talked to have found these enabling or even inspirational. Philip Brock of Evergreens, Hull, for example, went on a week-long course on making mosaics and came home eager to try out his new skills in the garden. Consulting your local FE – or other continuing education – centre may reveal resources you had not thought of.

An important source of both inspiration and know-how can be agreeably gained by visiting other people's gardens and talking to their creators. A very important resource in the UK is the annual guide book of the National Garden Scheme's Gardens Open for Charity (and its Scottish equivalent). Many of the gardens in this book open for at least one day a year under this scheme. There is a minor problem: the descriptive accent is always on flowers and plantmanship rather than underlying design or individual non-horticultural features, so the text needs some decoding if you are searching for wit and illusion.

Gardens open to the public on a more regular basis can be found through your local tourist information bureau, the public library, local newspapers or a good garden centre.

Creative gardening in the wit tradition requires originality, flair and boldness. But it also requires patience. For some years, Ken Mines has wanted to make his Kentish garden more interesting. He had some Victorian architectural features, but no real sense of direction. Recently he discovered Derek Jarman's garden at Prospect Cottage and Ivan Hicks' Garden in Mind. He sees these now as points of reference, not something he wants to copy but a new approach to materials and possibilities. Having reached this conclusion, however, he has become very clear that the next phase is to wait and see – but with a sense that he knows what he is looking for. Good ideas have to be recognized, absorbed and brooded over, as well as executed boldly when the time is right.

BUILDING

Earthworks

Almost all garden design of even the most traditional sort involves some sort of 'earthworks' – the laying of paths and the construction of steps, raised beds, a rockery or patio, for example. In theory, the creation of spiral mounds, caves, ramparts or amphitheatres is not very different. Most books on garden design, therefore, address many of the technical issues. Many garden designers will offer a consultation service, even if you do not want them to provide detailed plans; and local building or landscaping companies might also be willing to be consulted for advice about the practical aspects of such projects. Because water is so popular in all sorts of gardens, there are a great number of books on creating ponds and other water features, and a large garden centre will often have free specialist advisors available.

When Capability Brown started to create large-scale lakes for his clients, he developed a strategy in relation to the spoil: 'not a cartload in, nor a cartload out.' This is probably, in part, what inspired him to build so many mounds. It is a good strategy: if you dig out a pond or hollow, think first what you are going to do with the excavated material; if you want to create a mound, wall, rampart or other elevation, think about where you are going to get the earth from.

Depending on both the size of the project and access to the site, you can either dig by hand or hire earth-moving equipment. If the scale is substantial and you are not experienced, it may be worthwhile hiring a mechanical digger and driver. If you live in a rural area, it may be worth speaking to a local farmer – at certain times of year he may well be very happy to find a short-term commercial use for his machinery.

However you go about the digging, remember to remove the topsoil first. Guard it jealously, and spread it over the completed structure when you have finished.

Different types of soil are more or less stable, and you should give some thought to whether or not your structure will need a hard core – especially if it will have heavy use or be expected to carry weight. Often the subsoil will be adequate.

Plant your structures as soon as possible to avoid erosion. If you are digging downwards – particularly in an urban area – check for buried services and tree roots. If you are building

upwards, check the effect on overhead cables and your neighbours' views and light.

Built Structures

It is difficult to give much general advice on erecting buildings in your garden, which can range from purchased frames to architect-designed projects, from a marquee hired for the weekend to weight-bearing bridges. Only you know if you can do the work yourself, at both the design and the execution level.

Garden structures need not cost a fortune – often less expensive solutions may prove perfectly satisfactory. Cheap materials can be made to look more expensive by applying a variety of 'deceptive' finishes. A surprising number of the buildings in this book are in fact constructed from building rubble, breeze blocks or exterior grade bonded woods. These can all be painted to look like stone, wood, marble or, presumably, fur if that is the effect you want.

Do give serious thought to safety, and perhaps to liability coverage. This is particularly important if children will be using the garden. We are all aware of the lethal potential of many sorts of water features, but bridges, roof gardens, tree-houses or other elevated structures are extremely attractive to the young. Wooden surfaces can become very slippery, wood and rope do rot and even metal frames will eventually rust or loosen – they should all be checked regularly. Any structure fixed to an organic frame (such as a live tree) is inevitably prone to movement, and should be inspected frequently, particularly after storms.

Some structures require planning permission and others do not. Check your local regulations.

Architectural salvage

If you are interested in built structures in your garden – at whatever scale – it is worth investigating your nearest or best architectural salvage firms, which are listed in the Yellow Pages. These companies acquire an extensive range of merchandise – from old scaffolding and substantial building materials to features such as chimneys, tiles, old brick and stone, and window and door frames – usually from demolitions. Although there is frequently a 'jumble sale' element to these establishments, the cost savings can be enormous (a bit like the difference between a junk shop and an antique shop for interior fittings).

Moreover, exploring such places may generate new ideas. The 'silver' reflective planters at Scypen (see page 79), for example, are in fact portions of chimney flue liner. John Bracey bought the liner for the house, but it turned out to be faulty. Instead of having the suppliers take it away when they brought its replacement, he transformed it. The Braceys are committed to recycling, and this discipline seems to mean that John Bracey has developed a remarkable eye for the potential of materials. Making regular visits to architectural salvage yards is one very good way of stimulating this sort of visual and creative imagination.

Best of all become friendly with their owners. Once they know what you are looking for they will very often make efforts to find it, and to let you know what they have or expect to have soon. When Ivan Hicks first began to develop the Garden in Mind, he was amazed by how much material people just gave him once they knew that he would find a creative use for it.

EFFECTS

Trompe-l'oeil

This French term covers any form of visual trickery, such as 3-D murals or false perspectives, in which, by means of manipulating space, distance and plane, the observer is 'tricked' into seeing something other than the 'real'. *Trompe-l'oeils* have a long and honourable tradition in landscape and gardening, but have become somewhat neglected with the current emphasis on the 'natural'.

One major breakthrough that led to the exuberant development of Renaissance art was the discovery of the rules of perspective. In Western culture the rules of 'realistic' drawing are based on the observation that parallel lines appear to get closer together and objects appear to get smaller the further away they are from the viewpoint. These rules are now well

established and fully understood: most of us can remember from primary school learning to draw cubes on a flat surface, or tunnels with a tiny dot of light at the far end. Any elementary art class or teach-yourself drawing book will provide a simple revision course if you want one.

In the context of the garden these ideas can be applied in two different directions: a vertical surface can appear to be three-dimensional or present a receding view; and a view can be made to appear longer (by, for example, narrowing a path or reducing the size of objects along a vista) or, less commonly, shorter (by the use of slopes, widening a path as it moves away from the viewer or elevating a focal point above a path).

The human eye is very well trained in these rules and is therefore surprisingly easy to deceive. (It is training – blind people who have their sight restored have the greatest difficulty learning to apprehend distance.) Almost all Western eyes

perceive not just distance, but also relative size, angle, curvature, etc., if it is presented according to these rules.

You can now buy pre-formed 'fake' arches, colonnades, statues and other architectural features to fix to vertical walls, or you can construct your own using paint, trellis, plants or almost anything that takes your fancy.

When incorporating a *trompe-l'oeil* into your garden, it is worth thinking about the following points:

i) Maintain a consistent scale. Make detailed sketches of a mural and scale them up. Errors of scale – particularly where you are mixing three-dimensional objects with vertical (two-dimensional) effects – are quickly noticed and often irritate.

ii) Be very clear where the *trompe-l'oeil* will be seen from. A quick visit to your local art gallery may prove useful when considering this, but for the best effect you may have to 'control' – by means of planting, fences or other methods – the angle from which the feature will be seen.

iii) Blend the 'trick' into the 'real' garden. For example, grow plants around a mural, so that there appears to be continuity between the genuine and the fake.

iv) Render or otherwise smooth a wall before you paint on to it. For most (though not all) such effects, a smooth surface will make the illusion more convincing.

v) Check the suitability of your chosen paint and your chosen surface. An increasing number of paints are suitable for external use; all require surface preparation.

Light and reflection

The amount, direction and quality of light create moods and other visual effects. Most people are aware of this when it comes to interior decoration. Again there are a great many books suggesting ways of making a room feel larger, warmer, lower-ceilinged, brighter and so forth. These involve using different colours on their own and in combination, and the source of light and its reflections. Most of these suggestions can be applied in the garden.

Along with the colours of both flowers and hard surfaces, and the amount of sun and shade that you install in your garden, the deliberate use of reflection can create a different kind of *trompe-l'oeil*. Water can be arranged to reflect both light and images, but it will do so most efficiently when it is still, i.e. horizontal. Other reflective surfaces – notably mirrors – do not have this restriction.

Once again, the rules of reflection are fairly simple: a reflective surface will 'bounce back' the image at the same angle as the eye falls on it. Stand in front of a mirror – ideally one of those old-fashioned dressing table mirrors with a central section and two swinging side panels – and observe how what you see changes as you move either the mirrors or your head.

The position and angle of a mirror or other reflecting surface is therefore crucial. A mirror is less likely to deceive the eye if it is positioned so that observers are looking straight at it and consequently seeing themselves face to face. Very slight variations of angles create very different effects; it is worth experimenting with these before installing a reflective surface.

Like other murals, vertical mirrors will be most effective if their edges are disguised or softened in some way, or if they fill the whole of the observable surface. So an arch-shaped mirror will more convincingly appear to lead on to a further garden if it is given the sort of architectural framework that such a 'real' arch would have – roses growing over a 'real' arch before it, a frame of stone or brick, an actual hinged gate open or half open in front of it, or 3-D pillars painted on the wall either side of it.

Mirrors (of whatever material) also reflect reflections. A series of mirrors angled in relation to each other can be used to create ever more complicated effects – for example a mirror either side of a right-angled corner can create a visual square four times as large out of a small triangle. It is difficult to hide seams between two mirrors, however, and a solid black line will shatter any illusion; plants, statuary or other features can be used to disguise mirrored corners.

Don't forget that mirrors are made of glass: they can break, and broken glass can be dangerous. Make sure that your supplier knows what the mirror is for – they may have useful suggestions and there may be legal restrictions. Mirrors should always be fixed with great care and the surface that supports them must be stable and secure itself. Footballs and mirror *trompe-l'oeils* probably do not belong in the same garden. But there are alternative materials including tin foil, stainless steel, aluminium, and even (although they may reflect less light) very dark laminated surfaces.

Also remember that, although a reflective surface can enormously enhance the quality and quantity of light in a garden, it can also dazzle and burn. Unless blinding flashes and spontaneous combustion are an effect you really want, it is not advisable to angle your mirror directly towards the sun.

PLANTS

Lawns

The traditional British lawn is about the most 'unnatural' plant form one can think of. It is also one of the most traditionally treated, which is odd. It is not hard to do more exciting things with a lawn, such as mowing it in an unusual way. A traditional striped lawn requires a 'drum' lawnmower with a weighted roller. A non-traditional striped lawn can be produced by using a slightly different height of blade for the alternate stripes (change round at each mowing). In the same way, you can carve almost anything into a lawn provided the design does not require any lines narrower than your lawnmower – though rigorous right angles can be tricky.

Lawn grass is now sold in a wide variety of types, each with slightly different purpose and appearance. The recommendations on the packets tend to be rather unimaginative – think through what they might mean in terms of effect. And remember that 'lawns' can be constructed of other substances than grass: chamomile and Astroturf are probably the best known.

Turf

Behind every good lawn is good turf, but turf has other uses than creating lawns. It is a surprisingly effective material for eye-catching features and will grow at quite unexpected angles (including the vertical). There are some points worth bearing in mind:

i) The easiest way to make complicated, steep-sided turf features is to grow the grass through chicken wire, which will stop the whole thing washing off in the first downpour. The grass will grow and hide the netting very quickly.

ii) Larger structures, such as sloped turf roofs, are subjected to substantial loadings from the elements. The whole lawn needs to be reinforced and restrained from slipping. There are membranes and other systems that will do this. Investigate them.

iii) Grass needs copious amounts of water to flourish – it may be worth placing water-absorbent gel crystals or a suitable irrigation system within the structure, particularly if it is very narrow or pointed.

iv) Grass needs a fairly even exposure to light to grow well. This can be a problem with 3-D structures. If the structure

Water

Reflections from water work in the same way as other reflections – what is reflected depends on the angle of the viewer's gaze. But there is less flexibility about the angle of the water. The crafty gardener must therefore manipulate the point of view rather than the reflective surface; the water surface, the scene to be reflected and the location of the viewer must be positioned in relation to each other.

The darker and stiller the water surface the more accurate and reliable the mirror image will be. A pool so clear that you can see the stones on the bottom will not give good reflection; if the bottom and sides of the pool are smooth and dark, the reflective quality will be improved. This technique can also be used to make a shallow pool seem deeper.

The reflective qualities of moving water can create a dancing of light which is itself an effect worth exploring.

is small, it is worth building it on a base (rather than directly into the ground) so that it can be turned regularly.

v) Turf with enough soil to sustain it – i.e. soil at least 5 cm (2 inches) deep – can become very heavy. If you want a meadow or lawn on a roof, for example, make sure that the joists can support the weight, even when the grass is wet.

vi) When creating complex or elaborate designs think about how you will cut the grass – excessively intricate corners can create nail-scissor 'mowing' requirements.

vii) When designing a large piece of lawn art – such as a mound, turf wall or seat – it is a good idea to provide it with a hard core of rubble, old bricks or stones (or even broken bottles). This will not only save on good topsoil but also stabilize the structure and make it last longer. Many gardeners have found that spoil from the construction of a pond, cave or declivity has been the initial inspiration to 'carve' their grassed areas more excitingly.

Topiary

The traditional plants used for classical topiary – such as yew, box or privet – require slightly different treatment and you should read about their general care before you set out on a seriously ambitious scheme. The most important rule is to 'keep at it': it is difficult to 'reclaim' topiary that has been neglected for too long.

Wire frame topiary allows a wider range of plants. Ivy is particularly easy to use in this context, but there really is no obvious limit. Frames can now be bought in a wide range of designs, or you can make your own. They have to be quite sturdy as plants can be surprisingly strong. Jessica Duncan, for example, has used drainpipes rather than wire for the trunks of her topiary elephants, because of the size that she required.

Depending on the species chosen, you can either grow the plants within the frame and trim following its lines or you can grow the plants, usually a climber, up the outside of the frame and tie new growth in as it develops. Be ruthless with branches that do not want to co-operate. A surprising number of plants can be 'topiarized' to a greater or lesser extent. Experiment.

There are other ways of trimming or forcing plants into particular forms. Fruit trees have traditionally been extensively manipulated, espaliered, cordoned, pillared and miniaturized both for agricultural and aesthetic purposes. These methods can be extended to a wide variety of less expected trees. While there is a great deal of advice on 'pruning', it tends to be

directed at maximizing flowering rather than the creation of unusual forms. If you are interested in the latter, the following suggestions, based largely on advice from Ivan Hicks, may be worth bearing in mind:

i) The 'natural' form of any given species will affect what you can do with it. The wider your knowledge of trees is, the more effective your manipulations will be.

ii) If you pull two branches together and bind them, they will fuse with each other; thus two trees can be persuaded to grow as an arch with a 'single' tree above the apex.

iii) Keep at them. The earlier new buds in the wrong places can be rubbed off the better.

iv) The fewer leaves you allow a tree to produce, the larger each leaf will be.

v) Trees planted in a circle with the sideways-growing branches plaited or woven into each other will form a very secure and self-supporting structure.

vi) You can train tree branches around frames that are subsequently removed. Circle trees can be trained around a bicycle wheel; bay trees with spiral trunks are usually trained around posts.

vii) Pollarding (pruning trees right back to the main trunk) can create bizarre shapes and allow one to have species of trees that would otherwise be too big for many gardens. Standardizing, best known with roses and wisteria, can offer the opposite effect – making 'trees' out of plants that more often appear as shrubby bushes. Gooseberry trees, especially the large-fruited dessert gooseberries, are a pleasing example of standardizing.

viii) Growing climbing plants through trees – for example roses or clematis through fruit trees – has been extensively practised, but could be developed further. Growing trees through other trees – by twisting the trunks together – produces a fascinating effect. Hiding the ubiquitous hanging baskets in trees with a fairly open leaf growth can produce a strong block of colour in an unexpected place.

viii) Be patient: with all shaping and pruning the most important thing is to establish a healthy plant with a firm basic shape. Don't be tempted to indulge the plant too early.

Willow trees produce long slender and very flexible shoots. These have proven ideal for weaving – both alive and dead, or indeed in combination. Willow sculpture from cut (dead) withies has become very popular recently, and there are several courses available. Live, growing willow can also be woven to

make fences, tunnels, summerhouses or indeed statuary. Freshly cut willow shoots root very easily; they grow fast and often have wonderfully coloured stems in winter. They are extremely thirsty, however, and getting rid of a mature willow tree can be very difficult.

Now that we have such a wide range of plants so easily available it is time to start experimenting further with ways of trimming, pruning and otherwise bullying them to discover what effects we might be able to produce. Plants are for gardens, not gardens are for plants!

MATERIALS

Wood and Stone

Many garden books address the techniques of handling wood and stone in all their manifold applications. Hints on the construction and preservation of features made from these materials are easily available. The fact that your structure is radically different in appearance from those on offer in your local garden centre almost certainly does not affect the treatment of the material. The preservation of wood, for example, whether you are building a hollow wooden elephant or a traditional summerhouse, is going to be the same. Be bold in design and conservative in treatment.

Metal

Wrought iron is a traditional garden material, for obvious reasons – it can be formed into elaborate shapes and lasts for a long time. It is heavy and expensive, however, and requires an expert to execute original designs. It also rusts. Rusting can, of course, be used effectively, but if that is not the look you want, it is crucial to maintain the paintwork – modern gloss and matte oil-based paints make this a much easier job than it used to be, and such paints now come in colour ranges as complete as interior paints (though harder to locate). Old wrought iron work is increasingly hard to find at reasonable prices, but it is worth keeping a look out: one person's old junk is the next gardener's inspiration.

Stainless steel has great reflective power and can be used, eco-responsibly, in place of water. It will not rust, but will need cleaning. In direct sunlight it can become extremely hot.

Aluminium looks promising. It is often cast for a faked wrought iron look, but should be considered on its own merits

– especially its reflective qualities; however, suppliers do not seem to have much information about its behaviour in the garden. Garden railways experts have discovered that although it is lighter, cheaper and easier to lay aluminium tracks than traditional steel ones, they are more susceptible to thermal movement – buckling, warping or shifting; this would presumably prove equally true in other situations.

Lead has also been used traditionally – especially for containers. At the Porter's Lodge Lionel Stirgess has used a lead panel (beaten by himself) behind a waterfall, which gives a very distinctive effect – he says that it is not too difficult to manipulate; and because of its use in roofing, sheet lead is not hard to obtain. It is, of course, toxic and affects the water that comes into contact with it – hence the replacement of lead water pipes.

We have seen old scrap metal and junk of all kinds – pram wheels, scaffolding, old garden tools, even an ex-typewriter – used in gardens for structural support and ornamental features. Keep an open mind and an open eye.

Ceramics

Clay products, such as flowerpots, glazed tiles, terracotta pots, statuary and border edgings, have been successfully used in the garden for centuries. The one key question is 'Is it frost proof?' – which depends on the original clay and glaze, and on the firing method. If the vendor doesn't know or won't say, assume it is not.

If you want to make your own garden ceramics, you will need access to a kiln. Try consulting with a potter, who may be happy to rent you kiln space and will certainly have useful advice. The local school, adult education centre or college may also be able to help. Raku and pit firing don't require high-temperature kilns. Read up on them in a good craft book.

Mosaics

Mosaic work is an ancient art form capable of producing stunningly beautiful effects. The basic techniques, though often fiddly, are not difficult; nor need the materials be expensive.

There are three basic methods of making mosaics:

i) The Classic Direct Method. 'Tessera' (the Latin word for 'square' although there is no rule which says they have to be square), traditionally of natural stone, glass or glazed ceramic, are mortared directly on to the surface and subsequently grouted in. The two important things to remember when using this method out of doors are a) any damp will rot the mortar if it can get behind the tesserae; and b) mortar dries very quickly – only work a small area at a time.

Craft shops can supply pre-cut tesserae in all sorts of materials. Alternatively, you can make your own out of cheap glazed tiles, for example, although the ease of cutting varies enormously.

ii) Pique Assiette. From 1938 until his death in 1964 Raymond Isadore constructed a mosaic work that eventually covered both the interior and exterior of his house. It was made entirely out of broken bits of glass and glazed dishes, so his neighbours nicknamed him 'Picassiette', which translates simply as 'the plate thief'. In honour of his fabulous achievement mosaic artists adopted the term 'pique assiette' to describe mosaics made of broken glass and china (or other natural products such as stones and shells). Obviously this is the cheapest method, and can produce extraordinary and totally personal effects. You will need a remarkable quantity of old china, so start accumulating long before you begin the work.

iii) The Indirect Method. This allows you to design and execute your mosaic 'off site'; to lay it out and correct it if necessary before making a permanent commitment. It also gives a flatter, smoother finish, which might be valuable for, say, a mosaic path. This is technically more complicated, since you have to turn the whole design over, and it would be worth consulting a proper manual or attending some classes before you begin. Many books suggest using a plywood backing, but this is less suitable than concrete for a garden mosaic because of the danger of it warping under damp conditions. If you do use wood, it must be thoroughly sealed first.

Glass

As may be clear, we are fans of glass in gardens, as it brings colour, sparkle, reflection, refraction and magic – at an affordable price. In addition to mirrors (see pages 83–7) it has many applications.

Washed glass 'pebbles' in various colours are now commercially available – consult your garden centre or building supplier. They can make a stunning alternative to gravel in all sorts of situations. Glass bricks are also commercially available (often through bathroom specialists).

However, building stable external walls out of glass is not that straightforward – this might be a job for a builder.

Stained glass (old or new) not only throws remarkable colours into a garden it also has the advantage of being translucent but not transparent –you can have magical light and privacy at the same time. Bottles, particularly wine bottles, provide a free, recyclable, ready-coloured material, and can be inverted over posts for ornamental fencing; inserted into the ground for border edging; used as translucent building blocks or smashed up for hard core. Mrs Johnson at Alwalton makes plant containers by using a large nail to make a hole in the bottom of wine bottles (this is surprisingly easy to do, but you must use bottles with a large indentation in the base). Plants grown downwards through the hole can take on bizarre forms as they struggle to turn upwards; and the bottles themselves, suspended by their necks and hung from trees, provide light and colour and confusion – the effect is magical.

Fabric

Upholstery garden furniture is a problem. The sad fact is that it is very difficult to find garden furniture that is both cosily padded and weatherproof. Plastic is horrid to sit on, especially in hot weather, so if you want upholstered seating in the open air, a certain amount of carrying in and out is necessary (a trolley with pneumatic tyres simplifies this job).

The following ideas are worth considering. Modern camping and outdoor pursuit shops offer an extraordinary range of comforts – better and usually cheaper than garden centres. Backing a carpet with ground sheeting will make it dew proof – you don't have to bring it in on rain-free nights. Chair legs placed in tin cans, or even on can lids, will be likewise protected. Plastic bags inside cushion covers protect the pad itself – and the cover will dry quickly. Canvas awnings, umbrellas and tents can provide both sun and shower protection – for people and furniture. Sailcloth (from a ships' chandler) is often cheaper than purpose-sold garden canvas. The continuing success of the deck chair demonstrates that canvas has many 'garden worthy' qualities. Cotton hammocks – such as the Brazilian hammock – are far more comfy than rope ones: they dry out quicker if they get wet; are lighter and easier to move and don't need further cushions, mattresses or pillows.

'Real' furniture looks stunning in the garden – it may be worth the carrying. Outside ceramic and tiled armchairs or sofas can create this look, but they aren't as comfortable. Good household wood-framed, upholstered furniture is not designed for the garden: there is no real way of weatherproofing it in any

permanent sense. However, an old sofa you were going to dispose of may well have a couple of happy seasons in the garden, if you remember to cover it when it rains.

Synthetics

One of the saddest things about contemporary gardening is the willingness to use synthetic materials only to create second-class imitations of 'natural' materials. A plastic container, however well executed, will never look like a terracotta one – why should it? But while it makes rather inferior terracotta objects, plastic makes great plastic objects. Plastics are highly malleable, don't rot, are waterproof and weather resistant and can offer a range of colours beyond any 'natural' material. We need to break away from the idea that there is something inherently ugly about synthetic materials and start exploring what we could do with them, as we have inside the home.

Nylon thread is the nearest thing to invisible support that we have got. It is surprisingly strong. Objects suspended from nylon thread can appear to float magically.

For small-scale sculptures and particularly for brightly coloured high lights 'Fimo' – a synthetic modelling material, which comes in a remarkable range of colours – is very effective in the garden and much easier to use oneself than clay. Most craft shops can supply it.

POWER

Pumps

It is easy to forget that until this century all fountains and other water features were created and maintained without mains (pressured) water and without electrical pumps. All moving effects – and as this book has shown there were numerous and adventurous varieties of mechanical devices – were powered by hydraulic systems (the natural force of water 'seeking its own level'); by wind – the numerous references, especially in the 16th century, to wind vanes, pennants and flags suggest that the desire for movement generated considerable ingenuity; by crude man-power; or, less frequently, by clockwork. Gardeners working in the 21st century should give regular and unstinted praise to electricity.

None the less hydraulics – including siphons – do still offer an interesting potential, especially for recycling and energy conservation. The Mercys (see page 96) water their roof

meadow by recycling their bathroom water. It is conveyed from the first floor of their house, down underground and up again, entirely by natural pressure. All that is needed is enough water in the higher tank to force the water up the rising pipe on to the roof-meadow. (If the difference in height was sufficient, they could use the same water to have a spouting fountain in the middle of the meadow.) Natural water pressure can also be used to operate mechanical devices – as watermills and hydro-electrical generators demonstrate.

Steam, smoke, wind and clockwork are all still available as sources of power, but are not much used in the garden. Consider these resources. To be honest, however, their neglect is not really surprising because electricity is so efficient, flexible and accessible to most of us; and has so many applications.

Electrical pumps, both for creating fountains and for recycling water back through water-feature systems, are dealt with in detail in the many books available on water gardens; ready-made pumps with DIY instructions for installation are widely and cheaply available.

Lighting

Prior to the 20th century, the vast majority of lighting was by fire (candles, lanterns, etc.). Today, lighting remains one of the least explored, least imaginatively deployed aspects of the contemporary garden. This is a shame as it is a very flexible and creative medium that also enhances physical safety and security.

Of course a great deal can still be done with candles (glass flame protectors of various types are a good idea), fires and natural light. For example, both sunlight and moonlight create shadows. These can be managed surprisingly effectively when cast on walls and screens. However, for the maximum effect most people will want at least to consider electricity.

Electrical power offers an enormous range of possibilities, from a string of cheerful fairy lights in a tree at Christmas time to complex and elaborate designs, but the basic physical characteristics of light mean that very specific moods and atmospheres can be produced simply from the location of the light source.

i) Uplighting. A light at a low level shines upwards into a tree or other structure. Angle the light away from the dominant point of view to avoid glare.

ii) Downlighting (sometimes called moonlighting). The main problem here is organizing the cables so they do not look hideous in daylight.

iii) Spotlighting. This dramatic treatment needs careful management, but can be extremely effective especially when applied to sculpture or other architectural features.

iv) Silhouetting. The light source is behind the object being illuminated, so that it stands out in dark relief. There can be a problem of glare if the silhouetted object is too flimsy. The 1999 eclipse, and its diamond ring at totality, suggested further rather different effects that might be produced with the light source behind a more solid object.

v) Shadow. The reverse – the light source is placed in front of an object. This can be very effective if the shadow cast can play on a wall or other smooth surface – it works especially well with plants, or other objects that move a little in the wind so that the shadow dances with them.

vi) Oblique. If a light beam is projected along or at an angle to a feature, particularly an irregular surface such as a rough stone wall, the irregularities will be emphasized by deep shadow and sharp lights.

vii) Special effects. New devices such as fibre optic lights, which can be run through water, can create thrilling effects.

In all cases it is probably worth experimenting a bit with a light on an extension cord, as the strength of the bulb and the position of the light source can create very different effects.

Heat

Heat is also available via electricity. The advantages of this for greenhouses, conservatories and swimming pools does not need spelling out. By using a low-voltage system underground, around the base of particular plants, Michael Shone created tiny frost-free microclimates, which enabled highly tender plants to grow apparently 'naturally' in his Wiltshire garden.

'Fog' gardens, with their wraiths of magical mist, are usually generated by steam (although liquid gas, and/or very fine, high-pressured water sprays can also be used). The water is heated to vaporizing temperature – you do not actually need to have it boiling.

Motion-responsive switches

On page 48 we have discussed the potential of the motion-responsive switch for lighting, pumps, steam, kinetic art and for all sorts of other illusions and effects. Such switches are readily, and not too expensively, available from DIY shops. They are sold for use as burglar alarms and external lighting, but can

easily be installed for other purposes. Remote-control switches, such as those for unlocking your car as you approach it or for opening garage doors, could have similar applications.

Warning

For reasons of safety all outside sockets and connections should be waterproof. Circuit breaks should be fitted, and all mains voltage wiring must be in PVC-sheathed armour cable and buried at least 45 cm (18 inches) underground. Check with a qualified electrician if you have any doubts at all about your proposed scheme.

SPECIAL EFFECTS AND DECORATIVE FEATURES

Sculpture

The positioning of any artwork in a garden is very important. If you plan to make something for yourself, you will probably have strong ideas of what you want to do; however, most of the successful concrete statuary that we have seen is made in the same basic way.

i) Form a very basic shape out of wood, or if the proposed statue is very elongated and thin, out of metal rods.

ii) Crunch chicken wire around this frame. It is surprisingly easy to model – as Rupert Till's wire statues suggest.

iii) Cover the shape with old cloth or even newspaper.

iv) Apply the concrete, shaping the detail as you go.

You can 'age' concrete very effectively by daubing it with yoghurt, which encourages lichens to grow.

Almost any material can be used to make garden sculpture: old trees and branches can either be utilized as 'found art' or can be nailed, stapled or plaited together; or carved. Wood, like stone, can be painted (using masonry or external gloss paint) and varnished. However, with many materials (such as pottery and ceramics) it is worth considering how weatherproof, and particularly frostproof, they will prove. As with all weighty garden construction, including paths and steps, it is advisable to put down a layer of hard core under the proposed site.

If you know artists whose work you like, it may be possible to borrow a piece – many artists like having their work displayed. Do think about insurance, however, as garden theft is sadly on the increase. If you buy a work of art, check with the artist or gallery about displaying it outside – some materials and finishes will not survive.

Sound

If you want to install a sound system in your garden, it is possible to buy sealed weatherproof speakers. The alternative is to build them protective covers. The position of your speakers requires considerable thought, as people tend to move around more in a garden than in an interior room.

Experience seems to indicate that it is best to keep the actual system inside – you can use your own domestic system with a switch that redirects the sound to the garden speakers. If you have a convenient garage, summerhouse, pavilion or shed, you can install a separate system there. Obviously the same safety provisos apply here as with any other electrical device.

If you want to create 'natural' sounds – bird song or running water, for instance – you can buy continuous-loop tapes of many such noises from theatrical suppliers. Recording your own can be difficult without professional equipment.

Even without exterior power it is possible to have sounds in the garden. We have already mentioned a contemporary water organ (see page 49) and Aeolian harps (see page 109), but the range of sounds that can be produced by wind chimes or mobiles is remarkable – from the clonking sound of bamboo sticks, through bells, pebbles, metal rods and bottles to complex layered sounds made by mixing the materials. These are extremely easily constructed and can be virtually free.

There are also a number of plants that, teamed up with the wind, will create magical sounds of their own – bamboos and grasses are perhaps the most obvious examples. You will need quite a large clump to get a good result.

Mazes and labyrinths

Grass paths are hard to maintain in a high hedge maze because of the shortage of light – consider gravel or some other hard surface. With a turf maze there is a tendency for the unmowed and less trodden ground between the paths to rise and for the paths to sink. If you do not like this effect it is advisable to move the path slightly each season. If paths are narrow it can be difficult to mow right angles. Some lawnmowers are more efficient at this than others, and a strimmer may prove helpful.

On the issue of design there are now several books on both historical and contemporary mazes that might help to trigger your own ideas. The hedge itself needs to be high enough and solid enough to enclose the explorer; and arguably, the paths in between require a reasonable width for comfort. We would strongly recommend visiting some existing mazes and thinking hard about both the trimming and the space involved.

Sundials

Although the basic principle behind a sundial is a simple one, and almost anything can be used for both the gnomon and the dial markers, the construction of a scientifically accurate sundial is not straightforward. If you want a working sundial and are not thoroughly informed yourself, you will need to consult an expert.

Notes on the text

1. See Bushell, Thomas, 'Post-script to the Judicious Reader' in *An Extract by Mr. Bushell of … Bacon's Philosophical Theory in Mineral Prosecutions*, 1660, pp.21–2.

2. See Clark, 1898.

3. See Repton, 1795.

4. Alexander Pope, quoted in James M. Osborn's edition of Joseph Spence, *Observations, Anecdotes, and Characters of Books and Men*, 1966, 2 vols, p.606.

5. Henry Hoare, quoted in Woodbridge, 1970.

6. Joshua Reynolds, quoted in C.R. Leslie and T. Taylor, *Life of Sir Joshua Reynolds*, 1865, 2 vols, p.607.

7. See Loudon, J.C. *The Gardener's Magazine*, August 1831, vol. 7, p.392.

8. A selection of botanical introductions into Britain since the 16th century and now commonly found in gardens:

Species	Date	Origin
Apricot (*Prunus armeniaca*)	*c*.1542	China
Bear's Breeches (*Acanthus mollis*)	1547–8	Italy
African Marigold (*Tagetes erecta*)	*c*.1550	Mexico
Clematis (*Clematis viticella*)	1569	Spain
Tulip (*Tulipa gesneriana*)	1578	Turkey
Hyacynth (*Hyacynthus orientalis*)	*c*.1580	Persia
Sunflower (*Helianthus annus*)	before 1597	N. America
Nasturtium (*Tropaeolum minus*)	before 1597	S. America
Sweet Pea (*Lathyrus odorata*)	1699	Sicily
Red Hot Poker (*Kniphofia uvaria*)	1707	S. Africa
Pelargonium (*Pelargonium zonale*)	1710	S. Africa
Iceland Poppy (*Papaver nudicaule*)	1730	Siberia
Weeping Willow (*Salyx babylonica*)	1730	Euphrates
Magnolia (*Magnolia grandiflora*)	*c*.1730	N. America
Camellia (*Camellia japonica*)	1739	China

Species	Date	Origin
Rhododendron (*Rhododendron ponticum*)	*c*.1750	Gibraltar
Tree Paeony (*Paeonia suffruticosa*)	1787	China
Common Blush Rose (*Rosa semperflorens*)	1789	China
Hydrangea (*Hydrangea macrophylla*)	1789	China
Lupin (*Lupinus arboreus*)	1792	California
Chrysanthemum (*Chrysanthemum sinensis* x *indicum*)	1793	China
Dahlia (*Dahlia pinnata*)	1798	C. America
Tiger Lily (*Lilium tigrinum*)	1804	China
Wisteria (*Wisteria sinensis*)	1816	China
Choisya (*Choisya ternata*)	1825	C. America
Petunia (*Petunia nyctagniflia*)	1831	Brazil
Fuchsia (*Fuchsia fulgens*)	1837	Mexico
Forsythia (*Forsythia viridissima*)	1844	China
Buddleja (*Buddleja davidii*)	1896	China
Lily (*Lilium regale*)	1906	China
Blue Poppy (*Meconopsis betonicifolia*)	1948	S. Tibet

9. See Ward, 1842, p.47

10. See Jarman, 1995.

11. From an unpublished article by Anne Wareham.

12. See Cunliffe-Lister, private publication.

13. See King, Ottersen and Rose, *Gardens with Style*, 1988, quoting Elizabeth Tate.

14. J.W. Goethe, quoted in Bartholomew, 1996.

15. Milne, A.A., *If I May*, London, 1920.

Bibliography

Bartholomew, James, *Yew and Non-Yew; Gardening for Horticultural Climbers*, Century, London, 1996.

Billington, Jill, *Small Gardens with Style: A New Approach to Garden Design*, Ward Lock, London, 1996.

Brookes, John, *Room Outside: A New Approach to Garden Design*, Thames and Hudson, London, 1969.

Burnett, Frances Hodgson, *The Secret Garden*, 1909.

Chambers, Sir William, *Dissertation on Oriental Gardening*, 1772.

Clark, Andrew (ed.), *Brief Lives* or *Letters by Eminent Persons* as related by John Aubrey (1626–97), 1898, 2 vols.

Cunliffe-Lister, Susan, *Garden Guide to Burton Agnes Hall*, private publication.

Daniel, Christopher St J.H., *Sundials, Shire Album 176*, Shire Publications Ltd, Princes Risborough, Bucks, 1986.

Dierks, Lesley, *Making Mosaics*, Stirling Books, 1997.

Fisher, Adrian, *Secrets of the Maze*, Thames and Hudson, London, 1998.

Goldsworthy, Andy, *Wood,* Viking, London, 1996.

Goldsworthy, Andy, *Stone*, Viking, London, 1994.

Hill, Thomas, *A Most Breife and Pleasant Treatyse*, 1563.

Jarman, Derek, *Modern Nature*, Century, London, 1991.

Jarman, Derek, *Derek Jarman's Garden*, Thames and Hudson, London, 1995.

Jellicoe, Geoffrey and Susan, Patrick Goode and Michael Lancaster, *The Oxford Companion to Gardens*, Oxford University Press, Oxford, 1986.

Jellicoe, Geoffrey and Susan, *The Landscape of Man*, Thames and Hudson, London, 3rd edn, 1995.

Keswick, Maggie, *The Chinese Garden: History, Art and Architecture*, 1986.

King, Peter (ed.), *The Good Gardens Guide*, Bloomsbury, London, 1999.

King, Peter, Carole Ottersen and Graham Rose, *Gardening with Style*, Bloomsbury, London, 1988.

Leslie, C.R. and T. Taylor, *Life of Sir Joshua Reynolds*, 1865, 2 vols.

Marvell, Andrew (1621–78), *The Garden*.

The National Garden Scheme, *Gardens Open for Charity*, annual.

Page, Russell, *The Education of a Gardener*, William Collins Sons & Co. Lt, 1962, reprinted with new preface, 1983.

Repton, Humphrey, *Sketches and Hints on Landscape Gardening*, 1795.

Riley, Patricia, *The New Topiary*, Garden Art Press, 1991.

Ross, Stephanie, *What Gardens Mean*, University of Chicago Press, 1998.

Schama, Simon, *Landscape and Memory*, HarperCollins, London, 1995.

Spedding, J. (ed.), *Complete Works of Francis Bacon*, including *Of Gardens* (1625), *Sylva sylvarum* (post. 1627) and *New Atlantis* (post. 1627), 1886.

Stevens, David, *The Garden Design Source Book*, Conran Octopus, London, 1998.

Sidney, Sir Philip, *The Countess of Pembroke's Arcadia*, 1590.

Sylvestre, Joshuah, *Eden,* 1598, trans. from Saluste Du Bartas, 1584.

Symes, Michael, *Garden Sculptures*, Shire Publications Ltd, Princes Risborough, Bucks, 1996.

Thacker, Christopher, *The Genius of the English Garden; The History of Gardens in Britain and Ireland*, Weidenfeld and Nicolson, London, 1994.

Woodbridge, Kenneth, *Landscape and Antiquity*, Clarendon Press, Oxford, 1970.

Ward, Nathanial, *On the Growth of Plants in Closely Glazed Cases*, 1842.

Index

Acknowledgements

With warm thanks to all the gardeners we spoke to, both those we used and those we didn't, including:

Michelle Alles, London; Kenneth and June Ashburner, Devon; Jonathan and Jo Baillie, London; The Blees, Kent; John and Ann Bracey, Devon; Philip Brock, Yorkshire; Kay Buxton, Norfolk; Capel Manor Gardens, Middlesex; George Carter; Mrs Clark, Oxon; Richard Coles; Paul Cooper, Powys; Christopher St J.H. Daniel, Kent; Mary Doogan, Norfolk; Liz Draper, Dorset; Jessica and Peter Duncan, Devon; Richard Fort, Cambridgeshire; Frolics of Winchester, Hants; The Gibberd Garden Trust, Essex; Andy Gill, Whichford Pottery, Oxon; Ian Hamilton Finlay, Lanarkshire; Mr and Mrs Hattat, Herefordshire; Ivan Hicks, Garden in Mind, Sussex; Bill Holloway, Gloucestershire; Bernard Holmes, Essex; Jack in the Bush Gallery, Yorkshire; Philip Jackson; Charles Jencks, Dumfries and Galloway; Scott Johnson, Bridgehampton, NY; Susanna Johnston, Oxon; Andrew Kay, Cumbria; Margot Knox, Melbourne, Australia; Roger Last, Norfolk; Andrew Lawson, Oxon; Emma Lush; Mr and Mrs Macoll, London; Nan McAvoy, Washington, D.C.; Dr J.A. Marston, Devon; John and Lynn Mercy, Kent; Ken Mines, Sussex; Mr A. Myers, Northants; The National Garden Scheme; Sheila New, Dorset; Peter Osbourne, Lancashire; Chris Parsons; Hannah Peschar Garden Gallery, Sussex; Plant World, Devon; Ian Pollard, Wilts; Sue Prideaux, Surrey; Mr and Mrs Richins, Surrey; David Rosewarne, London; Andrew Sankey, Lincs; Les and Barbara Shapland, Devon; The Shone family, White's Farmhouse, Oxon; Mr and Mrs Siggers, Bucks; Michael and Elizabeth Stewart, Kent; Geoffrey Stinton, West Sussex; Jane Sutherland, Daedelus Inc., Norfolk; John Tordoff, London; The Trustees, Lamport Hall, Northants; Myra Tucker, Bristol; Rinus and Aniet Van de Sande, Devon; Anne Wareham, Wales; Barbara Watson, Peterborough; Mr and Mrs Whitehorn, West Sussex; Craig Wincoll and Lionel Stirgess, Suffolk; Judy Wiseman, London; Johnny Woodford and Cleve West.

We would also like to thank:
Kate Smith, Hope Maitland, Catherine Henderson, Will Anderson, Ralph and Sarah Grierson, Carol and Norman Hardyman, Slaney Begley, Adam Lee, Helen Fickling, Sam Boyce, Lisa Rawley, Bill Sterland, David Clarke, Jenni Bird, Brian Brown and Susan Crew.

Many of the gardens we visited were found through the National Garden Scheme's *Yellow Book*. We recommend consulting the most up-to-date edition for information on opening times etc.

Acknowledgements cont.

Text acknowledgements

The quotation on page 60 is from *If I May* by A.A.Milne. © A.A.Milne 1920, reproduced by permission of Curtis Brown Ltd., London.
The comments of Charles Jencks quoted on page 129 were made to Jane Owen, Gardening Correspondent of *The Times*, and appeared originally in *The Garden* (journal of the Royal Horticultural Society) in May 1998.

All efforts have been made to trace copyright holders, but if notified the publishers would be happy to rectify any omissions in future editions.

Picture credits

All photographs are by Peter Matthews with the exception of the following:

Mark Bolton: 82 (design: Sue Berger) Bristol
Nicola Browne: 90 (design: Keith Wiley) The Garden House, Devon
Bridgeman Art Library: 3 Flower Garden, Valley-Field from *Fragments on the Theory and Practice of Landscape Gardening*, (pub.1816) by Humphrey Repton; 18 Villa Pratolino (demidoff) from a series of lunettes depicting views of the Medici villas, 1599 (tempera on panel) by Giusto Utens/Museo di Firenze Com'era, Florence; 20 *The Pheasantry*, engraved by Joseph Stadler from *Designs for the Pavilion at Brighton*, (pub.1808) by Humphrey Repton; 21 Chiswick House Gardens (oil on canvas) English school (18th century) Victoria & Albert Museum, London; 25 *View in Kew Gardens of the Alhambra and Pagoda*, engraving by Heinrich Schutz, c.1798 after Franz Joseph Manskirch/Guildhall Library, London; 26 *Primavera*, c.1478 (tempera on Panel) by Sandro Botticelli/Galleria degli Uffizi, Florence
Richard P. Felber: 115 Kent, Connecticut, USA
Greenworld Pictures: 15 Mick Hales
John Glover: 50 (design: David Stevenson); 127; 133

(design: Alex Champion)
Georgia Glynn Smith: 81 (design: Billy Estes) Golden, New Mexico
Jerry Harpur: 47 below Ladlew, Maryland USA; 51 (design: Margaret Knox) Melbourne, Australia; 63 Green Animals, Newport, Rhode Island USA
Sunniva Harte: 37
Andrea Jones/Garden Exposures: 19 Villa Beatrice, Firenze, Italy
Andrew Lawson: 2, Stone Lane Gardens, Chagford, Devon
S &O Mathews: 104
Marianne Majerus: 54 (design: Judy Wiseman); 61 (design: Adrian Gunning); 64 Galarie Beaubourg (design: Niki de Saint Phalle); 67 (design: George Carter); 72 (design: George Carter); 85 (design: Charles Jencks & Maggie Keswick) London; 86 (design: Carter, Fulcher & Tate); 107 (design: Ivan Hicks); 128 (design: Charles Jencks)
Tony Mott: 45 Villa Medici, Pratalino, Italy; 46 Palazzo Orsini, Bomarzo; Italy
The National Trust Photo Library: 22 Andrew Butler
Clive Nichols: 23; 69 (design: Emma Lush) RHS Chelsea Flower Show
Hugh Palmer: 13; 17
Clay Perry: 113
Vivian Russell: 14; 32 Napa Valley, California
Derek St. Romaine: 56-57 (design: Johnny Woodford and Cleve West); 117 (design: Cleve West); 131 (design: Paul Cooper)
Deidi von Schaewen: 36; 39 Provence; 41; 29 Swarovski Crystal Worlds, Austria, giant water-spouting gargoyle (design: André Heller)
Holt Studios: Bjorn Ullhagen 66